C I T Y P A C K
Paris

By Fiona Dunlop

2ND EDITION

Fodor's Travel Publications, Inc.
New York • Toronto • London • Sydney • Auckland

WWW.FODORS.COM/

Contents

About this book

KEY TO SYMBOLS

✚ map reference on the fold-out map accompanying this book (see below)

✉ address

☎ telephone number

🕐 opening times

🍴 restaurant or café on premises or nearby

Ⓜ nearest métro (underground) train station

🚆 nearest overground train station

🚌 nearest bus route

⛴ nearest riverboat or ferry stop

♿ facilities for visitors with disabilities

✋ admission charge

↔ other nearby places of interest

❓ tours, lectures, or special events

➤ indicates the page where you will find a fuller description

ℹ tourist information

Citypack Paris is divided into six sections to cover the six most important aspects of your visit to Paris. It includes:

- The author's view of the city and its people
- Itineraries, walks and excursions
- The top 25 sights to visit—as selected by the author
- Features on what makes the city special
- Detailed listings of restaurants, hotels, shops and nightlife
- Practical information

In addition, easy-to-read side panels provide extra facts and snippets, highlights of places to visit, and invaluable practical advice.

CROSS-REFERENCES

To help you make the most of your visit, cross-references, indicated by ➤ , show you where to find additional information about a place or subject.

MAPS

- **The fold-out map** in the wallet at the back of the book is a comprehensive street plan of Paris. All the map references given in the book refer to this map. For example, the Musée du Louvre at 99 rue de Rivoli has the following information: ✚ 65—indicating the grid square of the map in which the Musée du Louvre will be found.

- **The city-center maps** found on the inside front and back covers of the book itself are for quick reference. They show the Top 25 Sights, described on pages 24–48, which are clearly plotted by number (❶ – ㉕, not page number) from west to east across the city.

PRICES

Where appropriate, an indication of the cost of an establishment is given by $ signs: **$$$** denotes higher prices, **$$** denotes average prices, while **$** denotes lower charges.

PARIS
life

INTRODUCING PARIS

The French state

An unmistakable characteristic of France and consequently Paris is the state's top-heavy role. Which other industrialized country allows a state bank (Crédit Lyonnais) to run up losses approaching 60 billion FF (US $11 billion) in five years? And which other nation offers amnesty to all traffic offenders when a new president is elected?

Paris remains the powerhouse of the nation, despite repeated government maneuvers for decentralization. This is where French socio-cultural trends are born, political battles are fielded, and national pride is polished. And yet it remains compact, still bordered by the *portes* (gateways) which keep the less prestigious *banlieues* (suburbs) at bay. Stay or live in central Paris and you are propelled into a maelstrom of gastronomy, fashion, cinema, literature, art...and monuments. History is omnipresent and no ruler —whether king or president—has failed to leave his mark on the city's urban face.

Philosophy, ideas, and culture have always been favorite Parisian preoccupations, but at this *fin de siècle* the momentum is slowing. The population is stagnating as inhabitants flee big-city life for less costly environs. Live here and you spend money: the temptations are multifarious and nothing comes cheap. New buildings prolifer-ated with President Mitterrand's *grands projets* of the 1980s; historic mansions are renovated, and state culture monopolizes every corner. Some say the city is becoming an asphyxiated museum, but spend a few days here and you cannot fail to be seduced by an enduring beauty, a grandeur, and a dynamism that few other capital cities combine.

Café life

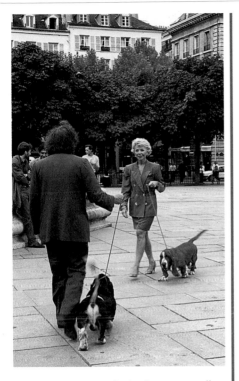

Place Saint-Sulpice, in the Latin Quarter

Paris still harbors a fascinating cosmopolitan character. Stroll from one *quartier* to the next and you make a minor global tour, taking in Africa, Asia, the Caribbean, and the Arab world in Pigalle, Belleville or the 13th *arrondissement* (area). Plunge into the heart of the French bourgeois soul in the 7th or 16th *arrondissements*, or sweep up Parisian chic on the Left Bank. Stop at a café terrace to people-watch, read, or dream; wander along the *quais* or collapse in a park.

Explore the Right Bank and you feel the capital's commercial pulse. Follow the city's cultural history in any of its numerous museums, catch up on new films at the countless cinemas, or dive into a hot nightspot. But above all let the city lead you and do not believe the cliché that Parisians are unfriendly. Its winding streets hold surprises that even the most informative guidebook cannot cover, and it is only off the tourist beat that you encounter the true Parisian spirit.

Incomparable Paris

"Paris is complete, Paris is the ceiling of humankind… Whoever sees Paris thinks he sees the basis of all history with a sky and constellations in between. Paris is synonymous with the cosmos…it has no limits. Paris does more than make the law, it makes fashion. Paris can be stupid if it wants, it sometimes allows itself this luxury… It is more than great, it is immense. Why? Because it dares."
Victor Hugo, *Les Misérables*.

PARIS IN FIGURES

HISTORICAL
(city growth)

- 1851: Paris represented 3% of the French population
- 1921: Paris population was 3 million
- 1925: Exposition des Arts Décoratifs drew 16 million visitors
- 1940: Germans occupying Paris saw only 25% of its inhabitants
- 1954: Paris represented 15% of the population
- 1954: 80% of Parisian homes had no bathroom
- 1990: 87% of Parisian homes had a WC

SOCIO-POLITICAL

- 10% of Parisians regularly attend mass
- 45% of Parisians go to the movies at least once a week
- An estimated 200,000–300,000 are homeless
- An estimated 150,000–400,000 are drug-addicts
- Parisians, forming 4% of the population, provide 45% of total income tax revenue
- 53% of Parisians use a car daily, 35% use public transportation
- The 1980s per capita cultural budget for Paris was 20 times that of the provinces
- 15% of Parisians are manual workers
- 30% of Parisians are executives or intellectuals
- 20 million tourists visit Paris annually
- 45% of Parisians live alone
- The Louvre had 6.3 million visitors in 1994
- 200,000 Parisian dogs produce 11 tons of excrement daily
- 800,000 French regularly consult a psychiatrist
- 90% of French women and 50% of French men use perfume

GEOGRAPHICAL

- 2.1 million inhabitants within the city walls (decreasing)
- 10.6 million inhabitants in the Ile de France (increasing)
- 52,000 inhabitants per square mile and an average of 1.92 per residence
- During July and August over 2 million cars head south
- 40% of street trees are plane trees
- 15,000 restaurants, cafés and clubs

Paris People

JEAN-PAUL GAULTIER

Now in his early 40s, Jean-Paul Gaultier is still a prime mover in the fickle French fashion world. After spending his formative years with *haute-couturiers* Pierre Cardin and Jean Patou, in 1979 he created his own label. From his first "James Bond" collection, through "Dadism," "Witches," and "High-Tech," Gaultier aimed to shock. Costumes for films, mobile furniture, a record, and TV shows in the UK have paralleled his two annual fashion collections.

Jean-Paul Gaultier

JOËL ROBUCHON

The man behind innovative Parisian gastronomy may be modest but his star still rises. In 1981 Robuchon took over a restaurant in the 16th *arrondissement*, and has not looked back since, accumulating gastronomy medals, writing books, playing French food ambassador, and confirming his status as France's top chef. He recently abandoned his restaurant in favor of becoming a roving *éminence grise* and to front a TV show on channel TF1.

ANNE SINCLAIR

An intellectual's sex symbol, chic TV interviewer Anne Sinclair has become the most popular woman in France in the last decade. Steering top personalities through their analysis of the week's events in her one-hour program, *7 sur 7*, this dark-haired, blue-eyed charmer has managed to extract declarations, confessions, hopes, and fears from such key names as Mikhail Gorbachov, Prince Charles, Madonna, and François Mitterrand.

PHILIPPE STARCK

Tripod orange-squeezers, chairs with pointed legs, a laughing TV—these are the hallmarks of Starck's design success. A "Made in France" phenomenon of the 1980s, Starck—gregarious, corpulent, and bearded—has presence in the 1990s. Still going strong is his redesign of the nightclub Les Bains Douches, while his latest gimmick is a mail-order house-kit composed of plans, a videotape, and a hammer.

Jacques Chirac

For over 18 years Jacques Chirac, the ebullient mayor of Paris and leader of the Gaullist party (RPR), surveyed the city from his palatial working residence overlooking the Seine, the Hôtel de Ville. With a taste for reading Chinese poetry (in French), he transformed the city's infrastructure and repeatedly clashed with the ruling Socialists until in May 1995, after two previously unsuccessful shots, he was finally elected president of France.

9

A CHRONOLOGY

c. 200 BC	Celtic tribe of Parisii settles on Ile de la Cité
c. AD 100	Growth of Gallo-Roman city of Lutetia
451	Ste. Geneviève saves Paris from Attila the Hun
1100s	Tragic love affair of Abélard and Héloïse
1163	Building starts on Notre-Dame
1215	University of Paris founded
1358	Royal family installed in Marais and Louvre
1337–1453	Hundred Years War between France and England
1430	Henry VI of England crowned king of France in Notre-Dame
1437	Charles VII regains control of Paris
1572	St. Bartholomew's Massacre ignites Wars of Religion
1600s	Paris reorganized; Le Marais developed
1648–1652	Civil uprising of La Fronde
1672	Louis XIV moves to Versailles
1700s	Development of Faubourg Saint-Germain
1789	Storming of the Bastille; declaration of Rights of Man
1792	Monarchy abolished; proclamation of the Republic
1793–1794	Reign of Terror; Louis XVI beheaded; inauguration of the Musée du Louvre
1804	Napoleon Bonaparte crowned emperor
1800–1814	Building of imperial monuments. Founding of Grandes Ecoles; increased centralization

1830	Bourbons overthrown, Louis-Philippe crowned
1848	Revolution topples Louis-Philippe; Second Republic headed by Napoleon III
1852–1870	Baron Haussmann transforms urban Paris
1870–1871	Paris besieged by Prussians, civil uprising of the Commune, Republic restored
1889	Eiffel Tower built for Exposition Universelle
1900	Grand and Petit Palais built for Exposition Universelle; first métro line opens
c. 1908	Modernism born in Montmartre with Picasso
1914–1918	Paris bombarded by German cannon, Big Bertha
1925	Exposition des Arts Décoratifs introduces art deco style
1940	Nazis occupy Paris
1944	Liberation of Paris led by Général de Gaulle
1954	National funeral for writer Colette
1958	De Gaulle called in to head Fifth Republic
1967	Les Halles market transferred to Rungis
1969	President Georges Pompidou elected
1974	President Valéry Giscard d'Estaing elected
1977	Jacques Chirac elected first mayor of Paris since 1871; Centre Georges Pompidou opens
1981	Election of President Mitterrand initiates *Grands Travaux*
1989	Bicentennial celebrations of the Revolution
1995	Election of President Chirac

PEOPLE & EVENTS FROM HISTORY

*Napoleon Bonaparte
(1769–1821)*

Henri IV

Authoritarian, complex and charismatic, Henri IV (1553–1610) was also Paris's first urban designer. In 1594, after renouncing Protestantism and uttering the legendary words 'Paris is well worth a mass', he triumphantly entered the city as a long-needed unifying force. His reign saw the growth of new industries, a fashion for châteaux, and the downfall of the peasant classes. Meanwhile, he instigated the building of Place Royale (Place des Vosges), Place Dauphine and the Pont Neuf, the rise of Le Marais, and the planting of 20,000 trees in the Tuileries before losing his life to an assassin's knife.

REVOLUTION

The Revolution of 1789 signaled the end of absolute royal power and the rise of popular democracy. The royal family was forced from Versailles to the Tuileries palace, but in 1792 this in turn was attacked and Louis XVI and Marie-Antoinette were imprisoned and sent to the guillotine. The year 1792–1793 marked the high point of the Terror, which was led by Robespierre, himself guillotined in 1794.

NAPOLEON

Napoleon Bonaparte's meteoric rise and fall from power (1800–1814) left an indelible mark on the capital. Ambitious reforms included the construction of neoclassical buildings, while his military campaigns made Paris capital of the greatest European empire since Charlemagne. More important was the increased concentration of the nation's culture and government in Paris, something that decentralization has still not eradicated two centuries later.

OCCUPATION

The scars left by France's Vichy régime were most apparent in Paris, occupied by the Nazis from 1940. Luxury hotels and public buildings were requisitioned, and Communists and Jews were deported in the thousands. After the Allies disembarked in Normandy in June 1944, a week-long insurrection by Parisians opened a path for them into the capital. General Von Cholitz capitulated after disobeying Hitler's orders to blow up the city, and Paris was reborn.

"LE GENERAL"

De Gaulle's role as one of France's major 20th-century figures started during the Occupation, when he headed the Free French Forces from London, continued with the Liberation, and was consolidated when he was called from retirement to solve the divisive Algerian War and head the Fifth Republic in 1958. His rule heralded increased presidential powers, a burgeoning consumer society, and the prominence of France within the European Union.

PARIS
how to organize your time

13

ITINERARIES

One of the pleasures of Paris is its compact scale and efficient public transportation. Visiting monuments in the central *arrondissements* is easiest and most scenic on foot and always includes obligatory café stops, but do not hesitate to dive into the métro for a short trip to more distant sights.

Moving between the monuments on Sundays and public holidays from mid-April to late-September is facilitated by Balabus, a public bus service that starts at the Gare de Lyon and stops at Saint-Michel, Musée d'Orsay, Louvre, Concorde, Champs-Elysées, Charles de Gaulle-Etoile, Porte Maillot, and Neuilly. The service runs between 12:30PM and 8PM and the whole trip takes 50 minutes. You can get off to visit a sight near a Balabus stop, then catch the next bus onward.

An alternative way of traveling around Paris between April and September is by a public riverboat christened "Batobus." Fares are paid either per stage or for the entire ride, which starts at the Port de la Bourdonnais by the Eiffel Tower and continues to the Musée d'Orsay, the Pont des Arts (Louvre), Notre-Dame, Hôtel de Ville (Centre Georges Pompidou), then returns along the same route.

ITINERARY ONE	LATIN QUARTER
Morning	Climb the tower of Notre-Dame (➤ 43) for a bird's-eye view over the city Walk beside the river to the Sainte-Chapelle (➤ 39) Cross to Boulevard Saint-Michel and walk up to the Musée de Cluny (➤ 38) Continue up Boulevard Saint-Michel to the Jardin du Luxembourg (➤ 37)
Lunch	Relax in the gardens and have lunch in a café near the Panthéon
Afternoon	Walk over to Eglise Saint-Etienne-du-Mont (➤ 52) Explore the winding streets that lead to the rue Monge Have a look at the Roman Arènes de Lutèce (➤ 59)
Drink	Walk south toward the Mosquée (➤ 52) and indulge in a mint tea Cross over to the Jardin des Plantes botanical garden and the Muséum National d'Histoire Naturelle (➤ 51)

ITINERARY TWO	STATELY PARIS
Breakfast	At the Samaritaine (➤ 57)
Morning	Cross Pont Neuf (➤ 55) to the island and take a boat trip along the Seine which returns to the island. Wander along the *quai* at river level to the Musée d'Orsay (➤ 31)
Lunch	Have lunch at the Musée d'Orsay, or walk up rue de Bellechasse and across Boulevard Saint-Germain to the Musée Rodin (➤ 29), with its rose garden café
Afternoon	Continue to Les Invalides (➤ 28) Visit the Eglise du Dôme (➤ 28) Walk along the esplanade to cross the ornate Pont Alexandre III (➤ 55) Visit the Petit Palais (➤ 27) Explore the Champs-Elysées (➤ 27) Catch bus No. 42 down Avenue Montaigne to the Eiffel Tower (➤ 26). Time it for sunset
ITINERARY THREE	GREEN PARIS
Morning	Start the day at the Musée Marmottan (➤ 24), then take the métro to Franklin-D. Roosevelt Walk down the paths of the Champs-Elysées (➤ 27) to Place de la Concorde (➤ 30) Cross to the Orangerie (➤ 30) Walk through the Tuileries (➤ 56), stopping for a drink at a kiosk
Lunch	Have lunch at the Café Marly (➤ 53) or in the Louvre's underground labyrinth
Afternoon	Visit a section of the Louvre's immense collection (➤ 35) then recover in the gardens of the Palais-Royal (➤ 59) Take bus No. 67 from the rue du Louvre to Pigalle, where you can catch the Monmartrobus to the top of Montmartre hill Watch the sun set over Paris from Sacré-Coeur (➤ 33)
Evening	Dine near the lively Place des Abbesses

WALKS

INFORMATION

Distance 2 miles
Time 1–2 hours
Start point Plateau Beaubourg
✚ H5/6
🚇 Rambuteau, Hôtel de Ville
End point Place des Vosges
✚ J6
🍽 Café Beaubourg, rue Saint-Martin; Ma Bourgogne, Place des Vosges (➤ 73)

Mère et enfant, *Picasso*

LE MARAIS TO THE PLACE DES VOSGES

After breakfast at the Café Beaubourg walk behind the Centre Georges Pompidou and turn right onto the rue Rambuteau, a colorful food-shopping street. Turn left up the rue des Archives, with the magnificent turreted Porte de Clisson (1375) rising from the Hôtel de Soubise (1709) on your right. Continue past a monumental fountain (1624) on your left and the Hôtel Guénégaud (1650)—which houses the Musée de la Chasse—diagonally opposite. Keep walking straight on to the rue de Bretagne, where you can rest in the leafy Square du Temple or investigate the leather-clothes market in the Carreau du Temple. Have a coffee nearby.

Along the rue de Bretagne, enter the picturesque food and flower market of Les Enfants Rouges (dating from the 1620s), then exit on to the rue Charlot. Walk south past the impressive Cathédrale Sainte-Croix-de-Paris, a former 17th-century convent, to the rue des Quatre-Fils. Turn left, past a new building which houses the National Archives, and continue to the rue Vieille-du-Temple. Circle round the garden of the Hôtel Salé, now home to the Musée Picasso, then continue to the Parc Royal, a small garden which is overlooked by a row of superbly restored 17th-century mansions. Take a look at the courtyard of the Hôtel de Chatillon at 13 rue Payenne, then continue to rue de Sévigné. Pass or be tempted by the fashion offerings of Romeo Gigli at No. 46, admire the two mansions of the Musée Carnavalet, then turn left onto the rue des Francs-Bourgeois. Carry straight on to the Place des Vosges and stop to have lunch at Ma Bourgogne.

PLACE DES VOSGES TO THE LATIN QUARTER

Walk through a passageway at No. 9 Place des Vosges to the courtyard of the Hôtel de Sully. Exit onto the rue Saint-Antoine, turn right and right again onto the rue de Turenne, then left to the charming Place du Marché Sainte-Catherine, good for a coffee-break at a café on a sunny day. Return to the main road and cross to rue Saint-Paul, lined with antique shops. Farther down on the right enter the Village Saint-Paul, a discreetly situated bric-a-brac market, then emerge on the other side into the rue des Jardins Saint-Paul. Here you see the largest remaining section of Philippe-Auguste's city wall. Turn left, then right along the rue de l'Ave Maria to reach the Hôtel de Sens, an exceptional example of 15th-century Gothic architecture. Look at the courtyard and the small formal garden behind the mansion. From here cross the Pont Marie to the Ile Saint-Louis. End your day in the web of Latin Quarter streets across the Seine.

THE SIGHTS

- Place des Vosges
- Village Saint-Paul (➤ 77)
- Philippe-Auguste's city wall
- Hôtel de Sens
- Ile Saint-Louis (➤ 44)

INFORMATION

Distance Approximately 1 mile
Time 1–2 hours
Start point Place des Vosges
✚ J6
🚇 Bastille, Chemin Vert, Saint-Paul
End point Latin Quarter, around Boulevard Saint-Michel, rue Saint-Jacques
✚ G/H6/7

Place des Vosges

EVENING STROLLS

INFORMATION

The Seine
Start point Place du Châtelet
End point Ile de la Cité
 H6
Châtelet

Bastille
Start point Place de la Bastille
End point Place des Vosges
J/K6
Bastille

*The Conciergerie at
the Palais de Justice*

THE SEINE
Start at Châtelet and walk toward the Louvre along the embankment opposite the illuminated Conciergerie, the Monnaie (Mint), and the Institut de France. At the Louvre make a detour into the Cour Carrée, magnificently lit and often deserted at night. Return to the river, cross the lively Pont des Arts, then walk back along the opposite bank, this time with views north of the stately Samaritaine and the Palais de Justice on the Ile de la Cité. Continue toward Saint-Michel, then cross over to Notre-Dame and make your way around the north side of the island, which offers views of the Ile Saint-Louis, the Hôtel de Ville and the Gothic Tour Saint-Jacques towering over the Place du Châtelet.

BASTILLE
From the Place de la Bastille walk up the rue de la Roquette until the road forks. Turn right along the bustling pedestrian street of rue de Lappe, which is packed with bars, nightclubs, and restaurants (keep an eye out for No. 71, a fine 18th-century house). Then turn left into the rue de Charonne. Pass art galleries and more bars before cutting back to the rue de la Roquette via the rue Keller. Notre-Dame de l'Espérance looms on your right, and at No. 68 there is a fountain (1839). Back at the fork turn right along rue Daval and cross two boulevards to rue du Pas de la Mule, which leads to the Place des Vosges.

ORGANIZED SIGHTSEEING

WALKING TOURS

CAISSE DES MONUMENTS HISTORIQUES ET DES SITES

Daily program of walking tours with lecturers.
✉ 62 rue Saint-Antoine 75004   ☎ 01 44 61 21 50/51
🚇 Bastille, Saint-Paul 🖐 Moderate

The **Ville de Paris** (municipality) offers guided tours to the Parc de Bagatelle, the Parc André Citroën, and the Père Lachaise, Montmartre, and Passy cemeteries.
☎ 01 40 67 97 00. Recorded information: 01 40 71 76 47

BOAT TRIPS

BATEAUX PARISIENS TOUR EIFFEL

✉ Rive Gauche, Port de la Bourdonnais   ☎ 01 44 11 33 44
🕐 Mon–Thu 10–6; Fri–Sun 10–9   🚇 Trocadéro   🖐 Very expensive

BATEAUX VEDETTES DU PONT-NEUF

Classic one-hour trip along the Seine.
✉ Square du Vert Galant 75001 ☎ 01 46 33 98 38 🕐 Daily 10–7 🚇 Pont Neuf 🖐 Expensive

CANAUXRAMA

Three-hour canal trip (part underground) between the Bastille and the Bassin de la Villette. Booking essential.
✉ Bassin de la Villette, 13 Quai de la Loire 75019 ☎ 01 42 39 15 00 🕐 Departures at 9:30 and 2:45 from Bassin de la Villette; 9:45 and 2:30 from the Port de l'Arsenal, Bastille 🚇 Jaurès or Bastille 🖐 Very expensive

BICYCLE TOURS

PARIS BIKE

Tours of Paris and further afield on mountain bikes (VTT).
✉ 83 rue Daguerre 75013 ☎ 01 30 51 87 64 🕐 Three-hour circuits and weekend trips 🚇 Denfert-Rochereau 🖐 Expensive

PARIS À VÉLO

✉ 9 rue Jacques Coeur 75004 ☎ 01 48 87 60 01 🕐 Short and long trips 🚇 Bastille 🖐 Expensive

Paris's canals

Cruising Paris's canals offers a more idiosyncratic view of Paris than the usual Seine trip. The revamped Arsenal dock at the Bastille (1806) is the kickoff for an underground vaulted passage which re-emerges at the Canal Saint-Martin. Chestnut trees, swing bridges, locks, the Hôtel du Nord (of celluloid fame), and modern apartment blocks lead to the Bassin de la Villette with its famous Rotonde (built by Ledoux in 1789). From here the Canal de l'Ourcq continues to the Parc de la Villette and then on eastwards for a further 67 miles.

EXCURSIONS

INFORMATION

Versailles

✉ Château de Versailles

☎ 01 30 84 74 00/76 18

🕐 State apartments: May–Sep
Tue–Sun 9–6. Oct–Apr
Tue–Sun 9–5. Grand and
Petit Trianon: May–Sep
Tue–Sun 10–6; Oct–Apr
Tue–Sun 10–5. Park: daily
7AM–sunset. Fountains:
May–Sep Sun 3:30–5

🍴 Cafés, restaurants

🚈 RER Line C Versailles Rive
Gauche

♿ Few

🎟 Château: expensive.
Park: free

❓ Guided tours

Vaux-le-Vicomte

✉ Château de Vaux-le-Vicomte,
77950 Maincy

☎ 01 64 14 41 90

🕐 Apr–Oct daily 10–6.
Nov–Mar daily 11–5.
Fountains: May–Oct second
and last Sat of month 3–6.
Candlelit tours: May–Sep Sat
8:30PM–11PM

🍴 Restaurant

🚈 SNCF Gare de Lyon to Melun,
then taxi

♿ Few

🎟 Expensive

❓ Guided tours

Giverny

✉ Fondation Claude Monet,
27620 Giverny

☎ 01 32 51 28 21

🕐 Apr–Oct Tue–Sun 10–6

🍴 Restaurant

🚈 SNCF Gare Saint-Lazare to
Vernon, then bus, rent a bike
or walk (3.5 miles)

♿ Good

🎟 Expensive

CHÂTEAU AND PARK OF VERSAILLES

Few tourists fail to visit Versailles, the ultimate symbol of French grandeur and sophistication, and the backdrop to the death throes of the monarchy. In 1661, when Louis XIV announced his intention of moving his court to this deserted swamp, it was to create a royal residence, seat of government, and home to French nobility. Building continued until his death in 1715, by which time the 250-acre park had been tamed to perfection by Le Nôtre. Hundreds of statues, follies and fountains, and the royal love nests of the Grand and Petit Trianon relieve the formal symmetry, while rowboats, bicycles, and a minitrain now offer instant relief from history. Inside the château, visit the Grands Appartements (the official court and entertainment halls), which include the staggeringly ornate Hall of Mirrors with painted ceilings by Lebrun. The Petits Appartements (the royal living quarters) display France's most priceless examples of 18th-century decoration and may be visited by guided tour only.

The Latona fountain, Versailles

VAUX-LE-VICOMTE

About 30 miles southeast of Paris lies the inspiration for Versailles, a château erected in 1656 by Louis XIV's ambitious regent and minister of finance, Nicolas Fouquet, who employed France's most talented artists and craftsmen. Five years later, a château-warming party of

The lily pond at Giverny

extravagant proportions provoked Louis XIV's envy and resulted in the arrest and imprisonment of Fouquet for embezzlement. Today, the interior and magnificent grounds have been entirely restored and include the Musée des Equipages (horse-drawn carriages) in the stables. Inside the château, resplendent with Lebrun's painted ceilings, do not miss the rich Chambre du Roi. In front of the château's neoclassical façade stretch terraces, lawns, fountains, and statues, these ending at a canal. If you have time, continue your stroll in the woods beyond.

GIVERNY

This small Normandy village is famous for one reason—Claude Monet. The painter lived in the village from 1883 until his death in 1926, inspiring a local artists' colony and producing some of Impressionism's most famous and startling canvases. His carefully tended garden with its Japanese-style lily pond gradually became his sole inspiration, and was as important to him as his painting. Only reproductions of his works are displayed here, but the colorfully painted house, his personal collection of Japanese prints, and the beautiful garden together offer a wonderful day out. May–June, when the borders are a riot of color, is the best time for the flowers.

Le Petit Trianon

The Petit Trianon, the jewel in the crown of French neoclassical architecture, was built for Louis XV's mistress, Madame du Barry, and later presented by Louis XVI to his wife, Marie-Antoinette (who was to utter the inept words "let them eat cake" from her royal chambers as the angry mob below clamored for bread). In a pursuit of the simple life, Marie-Antoinette transformed the grounds into a "wild" park, complete with a make-believe village where she tended sheep.

21

WHAT'S ON

Information on current events is best found in *Pariscope*, an inexpensive weekly listings magazine (out on Wednesday) which covers everything from concerts to cinema, theater, sports, and nightclubs; it has a useful section in English. *Figaroscope* comes with *Le Figaro* on Wednesdays and also offers a good round-up of current events.

JANUARY	*America Stakes*: at Vincennes racecourse
FEBRUARY	*National Rugby Tournament*
MARCH	*International Jumping*: at Palais Omnisports de Paris Bercy
APRIL	*International Paris Fair*: stands promoting gastronomy, tourism, and publications from all over the world
MAY	*Labor Day* (May 1): sees endless processions, thousands of bouquets of symbolic lilies of the valley, and no newspapers
	Armistice Day (May 8)
JUNE	*Fête de la Musique* (midsummer's night): crowds spring to life during this government-sponsored event, which schedules major rock and world-music bands
	Course des Garçons de Café (late June): over 500 waiters and waitresses career along the streets, each armed with tray, bottle, and glasses
JULY	*Bastille Day* (July 14): number one on the French festival calendar—celebrates the 1789 storming of the Bastille. Fireworks and street dances take over on the evening of July13, while the 14th itself is devoted to a military parade on the Champs-Elysées
AUGUST	Annual exodus and *Fête des quartiers*: outdoor concerts and street theater
SEPTEMBER	*Fête à Neu-Neu*: a fair in the Bois de Boulogne
	Festival d'Automne à Paris (mid-September until the end of December): music, theater, and dance performances throughout the city
OCTOBER	*Foire International d'Art Contemporain*: Paris's biggest modern art fair, at the Grand Palais
NOVEMBER	*Beaujolais Nouveau* (third Thursday in November): liberal amounts of wine are drunk when the first bottles hit Paris
	Antiques fair: at Pelouse d'Auteuil, Place de la Porte de Passy
DECEMBER	*Paris International Boat Show*: at the Porte de Versailles

PARIS's
top 25 sights

The sights are shown on the maps on the inside front cover and inside back cover, numbered **1–25** *from west to east across the city*

MUSÉE MARMOTTAN

HIGHLIGHTS

- *Impression—soleil levant*, Monet
- *Bouquet de Fleurs*, Gauguin
- Gold table-tray
- Geographical clock
- *Promenade près d'Argenteuil*, Monet
- *Charing Cross Bridge*, Monet
- *L'Allée des Rosiers*, Monet
- *Le Pont Japonais*, Monet
- Monet's water-lilies series
- Monet's spectacles

INFORMATION

- B6
- 2 rue Louis-Boilly 75016
- 01 42 24 07 02
- Tue–Sun 10–5:30
- La Muette
- 32
- RER Line C Boulainvilliers
- Expensive
- Bois de Boulogne (➤ 56)

One of the few incentives to get out into the residential 16th arrondissement is the Marmottan, where a mesmerizing collection of Monet paintings makes a welcome escape from the often colorless Parisian landscape.

Rich donations This often overlooked treasure of Parisian culture offers an eclectic collection built up over the years from the original donation of Renaissance and First Empire paintings and furniture given to the nation by the art historian Paul Marmottan in 1932. His discreetly elegant 19th-century mansion, furnished with Renaissance tapestries and sculptures and Napoleonic furniture, was later given an extra boost by an exceptional donation from Michel Monet. This included 65 works by his father Claude Monet, the Impressionist painter, as well as the stunning Wildenstein collection of 230 illustrated manuscripts from the 13th to 16th centuries. Works by Monet's contemporaries Gauguin, Renoir, Pissarro, Sisley, Berthe Morisot, and Gustave Caillebotte add to the Impressionist focus, but it is above all Monet's luminous canvases of dappled irises, wisteria, and water-lilies, dating from his last years at Giverny, that are memorable.

Shame It happens even to the best of museums, but when nine major paintings were stolen from the Marmottan in 1985 it caused acute embarrassment, not least because the booty included Monet's seminal work, *Impression—soleil levant*, which gave the movement its name. Five years later, after a police operation on a worldwide scale, the plundered paintings were discovered in Corsica. They are now on display once again, needless to say under greatly increased security.

Top: Impression—soleil levant, *Monet*

PALAIS DE CHAILLOT

With its majestic wings curving toward the Eiffel Tower across the Seine and its monumental presence, the Palais de Chaillot impresses. But it also has a human aspect: roller-skating heroes, mime artists, and Sunday promenaders.

Attractions The 1937 Exposition Universelle instigated the Palais de Chaillot's columns, these punctuated with bronze statues which overlook terraces and fountains. This spectacular art deco wrapping contains four museums, a theater, and the Cinémathèque Française. The west wing houses the Musée de l'Homme and the Musée de la Marine, the former catering to anthropological leanings and the latter to maritime and naval interests. A newly converted gallery at the Musée de l'Homme houses temporary thematic exhibitions, while the main collection gathers dust upstairs awaiting imminent renovation. On the top floor is the Salon de la Musique, which displays some 500 "world" musical instruments used for Sunday concerts.

Illusions In the building's east wing nestles an extraordinary museum, the Musée des Monuments Français, conceived by the 19th-century medievalist architect, Viollet-le-Duc. Full-scale replicas and casts of French architectural fea-

An exhibit in the marine museum

tures from pre-Roman times to the 19th century include gargoyles, frescoes, stained glass, statues, and even a fountain. More replicas of reality can be found in the adjoining Musée du Cinéma, which traces the evolution of filmmaking through early movie cameras, sets, and costumes.

HIGHLIGHTS

- Napoleon's imperial barge
- *Ports de France*, Vernet
- *Le Valmy*
- African frescoes
- Javanese *gamelan* orchestra
- King Béhanzin
- Reproduction of Saint-Savin-sur-Gartempe
- Baroque fountain
- Fritz Lang's robot
- Rudolf Valentino costume

INFORMATION

- ✚ D5
- ✉ Place du Trocadéro 75016
- ☎ Marine: 01 45 53 31 70. Homme: 01 44 05 72 72. Monuments: 01 44 05 39 05. Cinéma: 01 45 53 74 39
- 🕐 Marine: Wed–Mon 10–6. Homme: Wed–Mon 9.45–5.15. Monuments: Wed–Mon 10–6. Cinéma: by guided tour only, Wed–Sun 10, 11, 2, 3, 4, 5 (phone to book)
- 🍴 Le Totem restaurant in the west wing
- Ⓜ Trocadéro
- 🚌 22, 30, 32, 63
- ♿ Few
- Moderate
- ↔ Musée d'Art Moderne de la Ville de Paris (▶ 50)
- ❓ Guided tours of Marine on request; ethnological films at Homme Sat–Sun 2:30

TOUR EIFFEL

- Panoramic views
- Bust of Gustave Eiffel

DID YOU KNOW?

- Weight: over 7,700 tons
- Made of 15,000 iron sections
- Height: 1,050 feet
- Top platform at 906 feet
- 1,652 steps to the top
- 55 tons of paint needed to repaint it
- 370 suicides

INFORMATION

- ✚ D6
- ✉ Champ de Mars 75007
- ☎ 01 44 11 23 45
- 🕐 Sep–Jun daily 9AM–11PM. Jul–Aug daily 9:30AM–midnight
- 🍴 La Belle France (1st floor ☎ 01 45 55 20 04), Jules Verne (2nd floor ☎ 01 45 55 61 44)
- Ⓜ Bir-Hakeim
- 🚌 42, 82
- 🚆 RER Line C, Tour Eiffel
- ♿ Very good (to 2nd floor)
- 🎧 Very expensive; stairs cheap
- ↔ Les Invalides (➤ 28)

The Eiffel Tower could be a cliché but it isn't. The powerful silhouette of Gustave Eiffel's marvel of engineering still makes a stirring sight, especially at night when its delicate, lace-like iron structure comes to the fore.

Glittering feat Built in a record two years for the 1889 Exposition Universelle, the controversial Eiffel Tower was never intended to be a permanent feature of the city. However, in 1910 it was finally saved for posterity, so preparing the way for today's 4 million annual visitors. Avoid long lines for the elevator by visiting the tower at night, when it fully lives up to its romantic image and provides a glittering spectacle—whether the 292,000-watt illumination of the "staircase to infinity" itself, or the carpet of nocturnal Paris unfolding at its feet.

Violent reactions Gustave Eiffel was a master of cast-iron structures, his prolific output including hundreds of factories, churches, railroad viaducts, and bridges on four continents. His 1,050-foot tower attracted great opposition, but his genius was vindicated by the fact that it sways no more

than 5 inches in high winds and remained the world's highest structure for 40 years. Eiffel kept an office here until his death in 1923; from it he may have seen Comte de Lambert circle above in a flying-machine in 1909, or a less fortunate Icarus plummet to his death from the parapet in 1912.

CHAMPS-ELYSÉES & ARC DE TRIOMPHE

You may not be enamoured of fast-food outlets and airline offices, both of which are major features of this once-glamorous avenue. But a recent face-lift has upgraded it, and nothing can change the magnificent east–west perspective.

Slow start It was Marie de Médicis, wife of Henri IV, who first made this a fashionable boulevard in 1616, but it was the celebrated landscape designer André Le Nôtre who contributed to its name—Elysian Fields—by planting alleys of trees and gardens. The heyday came in 1824 when new sidewalks and fountains made it the most fashionable promenading spot in Paris, with cafés and restaurants catering to a well-heeled clientele. Crowning the cake was the Arc de Triomphe (►57), commissioned by Napoleon, while the 1900 Exposition Universelle added the glass and iron domes of the Grand Palais (which includes the Palais de la Découverte) and the Petit Palais at the lower end.

Parades Despite being dominated by commercial and tourist facilities, the Champs-Elysées remains the symbolic focal point for national ceremonies, whether the traditional July 14 military parade, Armistice Day's wreath-laying at the Arc de Triomphe, or the fast-pedaling *grande finale* of the Tour de France. A recent highlight was the 1989 Bicentennial procession, when Jessye Norman led a spectacular host of swaying performers down to the Place de la Concorde.

Luxury These days the Champs-Elysées may be dominated by car showrooms, but plush cinemas, upscale stores, and one or two fashionable watering holes still remain to tempt those who want to see and be seen.

HIGHLIGHTS

- Arc de Triomphe
- Rude's "Marseillaise" sculpture on Arc de Triomphe
- L'Etoile
- Bluebell Girls at Lido
- Fouquets restaurant
- Palais de l'Elysée
- Ledoyen restaurant
- Grand Palais
- Petit Palais
- Philatelists' market

INFORMATION

- ✚ D4
- ✉ Champs-Elysées 75008
- ☎ Grand Palais: 01 44 13 17 17. Petit Palais: 01 42 65 12 73. Découverte: 01 40 74 81 82
- 🕐 Grand Palais: Wed–Mon 10–8. Petit Palais: Tue–Sun 10–5:40. Palais de la Découverte: Tue–Sat 9:30–6; Sun 10–7
- 🍴 Grand Palais: average cafeteria. Cafés and restaurants on Champs-Elysées
- 🚇 Charles de Gaulle-Etoile, Georges V, Franklin-D. Roosevelt, Champs-Elysées-Clémenceau
- 🚌 32, 42, 73
- ♿ Good
- 💵 Moderate to expensive
- ↔ Place de la Concorde (►30)
- ❓ Photo library and scientific films in Palais de la Découverte

27

5

LES INVALIDES

HIGHLIGHTS

- 643-foot façade
- Sword and armor of François I
- Salle Orientale
- Napoleon's stuffed horse
- *Emperor Napoleon*, Ingres
- Galerie des Plans-Reliefs
- Napoleon's tomb
- Dome
- 17th-century organ
- A Renault light tank

INFORMATION

- ✚ E6
- ✉ Esplanade des Invalides 75007
- ☏ Musée de l'Armée: 01 44 42 37 67
- 🕐 Oct–Mar daily 10–5. Apr–Sep daily 10–6
- 🚇 La Tour Maubourg, Invalides, Varenne
- 🚌 28, 49, 69, 82, 92
- 🚆 RER Line C Invalides
- ♿ Good
- 💰 Expensive
- ↔ Musée Rodin (➤ 29)
- ❓ Guided tours on request ☏ 01 45 51 95 05; films on World Wars I and II

The gilded dome rising above the Hôtel des Invalides is reminiscent of the pomp and glory of France's two greatest promoters— the Sun King, who built Les Invalides, and the power-hungry Napoleon Bonaparte, who is entombed there.

Glory The vast, imposing edifice of Les Invalides was built to house invalid soldiers, and it continues to accommodate a handful today. Its classical façade and majestic Cour d'Honneur date from the 1670s, with the ornate Eglise du Dôme completed in 1706 and the long grassy esplanade established soon after. Home to military institutions, Les Invalides is also a memorial to the endless battles and campaigns that have marked French history and which are extensively illustrated in the Musée de l'Armée. Here you can trace the evolution of warfare from early days to World War II, and there are daily screenings of war films.

The Cour d'Honneur

Tombs There are more relics inside the Eglise Saint-Louis, where tattered enemy standards hang despondently from cornices, but it is above all the baroque cupolas, arches, columns, and sculptures of the Eglise du Dôme that highlight France's military achievements and heroes. Tombs of generals fill the chapels while the circular crypt contains Napoleon's grandiose sarcophagus (which incorporates six successive layers), guarded by 12 statues, symbols of his military campaigns.

MUSÉE RODIN

As a complete antidote to the military might of Les Invalides, wander into the enchanting Musée Rodin, often forgotten by Parisians. This surprisingly peaceful enclave lifts you out of the hurly-burly of the boulevards into another sphere.

Hard times This rococo mansion, built for a prosperous wig-maker in 1730, has a checkered history. One owner (Maréchal de Biron) was sent to the guillotine, and the house has been used successively as a dance hall, convent, school, and as artists' studios. Rodin lived here from 1908 until his death in 1917, with such neighbors as the poet Rainer Maria Rilke and dancer Isadora Duncan. In 1919 the house was transformed into a museum.

Sculpture The elegant, luminous interior houses the collection of works that Rodin left to the nation on his death in 1917. It ranges from his early academic sketches to the later water-colors, and displays many of his most celebrated white marble and bronze sculptures, including *The Kiss*. There are busts of the composer Mahler, the suffragette Eva Fairfax, and Victor Hugo to name but a few, as well as a series of studies of Balzac in paunchy splendor. Alongside the Rodins are works by his contemporaries, in particular his tragic mistress and model, Camille Claudel, as well as Eugène Carrière, Munch, Renoir, Monet, and Van Gogh. Rodin's furniture and antiques complete this exceptional collection.

Retreat The museum's private gardens are Paris's third largest and contain several major sculptures, a pond, flowering shrubs, benches for a quiet read, a converted chapel used for temporary exhibitions, and an open-air café.

HIGHLIGHTS

- Les Bourgeois de Calais
- Le Penseur
- La Porte de l'Enfer
- Le Baiser
- La Main de Dieu
- Saint Jean Baptiste
- Adam et Eve
- Ugolin
- Le Père Tanguy, Van Gogh
- Original staircase

INFORMATION

- F6
- 77 rue de Varenne 75007
- 01 47 05 01 34
- Winter Tue–Sun 9:30–4:45. Summer Tue–Sun 9:30–5:45
- Peaceful garden café
- Varenne
- 69
- Good
- Moderate
- Les Invalides (► 28)

PLACE DE LA CONCORDE

HIGHLIGHTS

- *Les Nymphéas*, Monet
- Jeu de Paume
- Hieroglyphs
- Hôtel Crillon
- *Chevaux de Marly*
- View up the Champs-Elysées

DID YOU KNOW?

- The Egyptian obelisk weighs 250 tons
- 133 people were trampled to death here in 1770
- 1,300 heads were guillotined here in 1793–1795

INFORMATION

- ✚ F5
- ✉ Place de la Concorde 75008
- ☎ Jeu de Paume: 01 47 03 12 50.
  Orangerie: 01 42 97 48 16
- 🕐 Jeu de Paume: Wed–Fri noon–7; Tue noon–9:30; Sat–Sun 10–7.
  Orangerie: Wed–Mon 9:45–5:15
- 🍴 Small designer café in Jeu de Paume
- Ⓜ Concorde
- 🚌 24, 42, 52, 72, 73, 84, 94
- ♿ Jeu de Paume: excellent Orangerie: none
- 💲 Moderate to expensive
- ↔ Champs-Elysées & Arc de Triomphe (➤ 27), Jardin des Tuileries (➤ 56)

As you stand in this noisy traffic-choked square it is hard to imagine the crowds baying for the deaths of Marie-Antoinette and Louis XVI, who were both guillotined here at the height of the Terror of the French Revolution.

Chop-chop This pulsating square was initially laid out in 1775 to accommodate a statue of King Louis XV. Under the new name of Place de la Révolution, it then witnessed the mass executions of the French Revolution, and was finally renamed the Place de la Concorde in 1795 as revolutionary zeal abated. In the 19th century, Guillaume Coustou's *Chevaux de Marly* were erected at the base of the Champs-Elysées (those you see today are reproductions, the originals now being housed in the Louvre). Crowning the center of the Concorde is a 3,000-year-old Egyptian obelisk overlooking eight symbolic statues of French cities. Dodging the traffic to have a closer look is to dice with death, but plans to ease the pedestrian's lot are currently under consideration.

Grandeur To the north, bordering the rue Royale, stand the colonnaded Hôtel Crillon (on the left) and the matching Hôtel de la Marine (right), both relics from pre-Revolutionary days. The rue Royale itself, with its luxury establishments, leads to the Madeleine. The eastern side of the Concorde is dominated by two public art galleries: the Jeu de Paume (by rue de Rivoli), which displays contemporary art exhibitions; and the Orangerie (nearer the river), famous for its impressive basement panels of Monet's *Water Lilies* and rather second-rate Impressionist paintings. Visible across the bridge to the south is the Palais Bourbon, home to the Assemblée Nationale (French parliament).

MUSÉE D'ORSAY

You'll either love or hate this conversion of a turn-of-the-century train station, but whatever your view its art collections, covering the years 1848–1914, are a must for anyone interested in the output of this crucial period.

Monolithic When this museum finally opened in 1986 controversy ran high: Gae Aulenti's heavy stone structures lay unhappily under Laloux's delicate iron and glass shell, built as a train terminus in 1900. But the collections redeem this *faux pas*, offering a solid overview of the momentous period from Romanticism to Fauvism. Ignore the monolithic mezzanine blocks and, after exploring the 19th-century

paintings, sculptures, and decorative arts on the ground floor, take the front escalator to the upper level. Here the Pont-Aven, Impressionist, and Nabis schools are displayed along with the giants of French art—Cézanne, Monet, Renoir, Van Gogh, Degas, Sisley, and Pissaro. And don't

The Church at Auvers, *Van Gogh*

miss the views from the outside terrace and café behind the station clock at the top.

To the ball The middle level is devoted to painting (Symbolism and Naturalism) and sculpture from 1870 to 1914, and it includes works by Rodin, Bourdelle, and Maillol. In the spectacular ballroom hang paintings by Gérôme and Bouguereau.

HIGHLIGHTS

- *Olympia*, Manet
- *Déjeuner sur l'Herbe*, Manet
- *Orphée*, Gustave Moreau
- *La Mère*, Whistler
- *L'Angélus du Soir*, Millet
- *La Cathédrale de Rouen*, Monet
- *L'Absinthe*, Degas
- *La Chambre à Arles*, Van Gogh
- *Femmes de Tahiti*, Gauguin
- Chair by Charles Rennie Mackintosh

INFORMATION

- ✛ F6
- ✉ 1 rue de Bellechasse 75007
- ☎ 01 40 49 48 14; 01 40 49 48 48
- 🕐 Tue–Sun 10–5:45, except Thu 10–9:30
- 🍴 Café des Hauteurs for good snacks; plush restaurant/ tea room in ballroom
- 🚇 Solférino
- 🚌 24, 68, 69
- 🚆 RER Linc C Musée d'Orsay
- ♿ Excellent
- 💲 Expensive
- ↔ Musée du Louvre (▶ 35)
- ❓ Audio and guided tours; pedagogical activities, concerts, and lectures

OPÉRA DE PARIS

HIGHLIGHTS

- Grand Escalier
- Grand Foyer
- *Apollo*, Millet
- Façade
- Lamp-bearers

DID YOU KNOW?

- Garnier's design was selected from 171 others
- The total surface area of the building is 118,400 square feet
- The auditorium holds 2,200 spectators
- The stage accommodates over 450 performers

INFORMATION

- ✚ G4
- ✉ Place de l'Opéra 75009
- ☎ Monument: 01 40 01 19 70.
  Bookings: 01 44 73 13 00.
  Museum: 01 47 42 07 02
- 🕐 Daily 10–4:30
- 🍴 Bar open during shows
- Ⓜ Opéra
- 🚌 20, 21, 22, 27, 29, 42, 52, 53, 66, 68, 81, 95
- 🚉 RER Auber
- ♿ Few, call for appointment
- 💷 Moderate
- ↔ Place de la Concorde (► 30)
- ❓ Guided tours daily at 1 PM except Mon; exhibitions

This is an ornate wedding cake of a building, but the sumptuous and riotous details that decorate its every surface are in fact the perfect epitaph to the frenetic architectural activities of the Second Empire.

Past glory When Charles Garnier's opera house was inaugurated in 1875 it marked the end of Haussmann's ambitious urban face-lift and announced the sociocultural buildup to the Belle Epoque, with Nijinsky and Diaghilev's Ballets Russes as later highlights. Today the Salle Garnier mostly stages dance with only some opera, many prestigious operatic performances having been switched to the Opéra Bastille when the latter opened in 1989. Rudolf Nureyev was director of the Paris Ballet here between 1983 and 1989, and this was where he first danced in the West. The brilliant dancer Patrick Dupond has steered the national ballet company fairly traditionally since 1990.

Dazzle Competing with a series of provocative lamp-bearing statues, the Palais Garnier's extravagant façade of arches, winged horses, friezes, and columns is topped by a copper-green dome and leads into a majestic foyer. This is dominated by the Grand Escalier, dripping with balconies and chandeliers, in turn sweeping upward to the Grand Foyer and its gilded mirrors, marble, murals, and Murano glass. Do not miss the equally ornate auditorium, with its dazzling gold-leaf decorations and red-velvet seats, and Marc Chagall's incongruous false ceiling, painted in 1964. The Opéra is open outside rehearsals (your best bet is 1–2PM); to visit, enter through Riccardo Pedruzzi's very 1990s library and the museum of operatic memorabilia.

SACRÉ-COEUR

Few people would admit it, but the high point of a trip up here is not the basilica itself but the stunning views. You can't forget, however, that Sacré-Coeur was built in honor of the 58,000 dead of the Franco–Prussian War.

Weighty Although construction started in 1875, it was not until 1914 that this white neo-Romanesque-Byzantine edifice was completed, partly due to the problems of building foundations in the quarry-riddled hill of Montmartre. Priests still work in relays to maintain the tradition of perpetual prayer for forgiveness of the horrors of war and for the massacre of some 20,000 Communards by government troops.

The square bell tower was an afterthought and houses one of the world's heaviest bells, La Savoyarde, which weighs in at 21 tons. The stained-glass windows are replacements of those that were shattered by enemy bombs in 1944.

Byzantine mosaic of Christ, chancel vault

Panoramas This unmistakable feature of the Paris skyline magnetizes the crowds arriving either by funicular or via the steep steps of the terraced garden. Dawn and dusk offer sparkling panoramas over the city, especially from the exterior terrace of the dome, the second-highest point in Paris after the Eiffel Tower (access is from the left-hand side of the basilica). Just to the east of Sacré-Coeur is the diminutive Saint-Pierre, a much reworked though charming church which is all that remains of the Benedictine abbey of Montmartre founded in 1133.

HIGHLIGHTS

- La Savoyarde bell
- View from the dome
- Mosaic of Christ
- Treasure of Sacré-Coeur
- Bronze doors at Saint-Pierre
- Stained-glass gallery
- Statue of Christ
- Statue of Virgin Mary and Child
- The funicular ride from Abbesses métro station

INFORMATION

- H3
- 35 rue Chevalier de la Barre 75018
- 01 53 41 89 00
- Basilica: daily 7AM–11PM. Dome and crypt: Apr–Sep daily 9–7. Oct–Mar daily 9–6
- Abbesses, then funicular
- Montmartrobus from Pigalle or Abbesses
- Few
- Basilica: free. Dome and crypt: cheap
- Montmartre Village (rue Lepic, Vineyard of Montmartre, Place des Abbesses)

Musée des Arts Décoratifs

HIGHLIGHTS

- Sculpted wood panels
- Reveillon wallpaper designs
- Bronze and wood cradle
- Dufour Leroy wallpaper
- Empress Joséphine's tea service
- Georges Hoentschell woodwork
- Jeanne Lanvin's apartment
- Glass radiator
- Martin Szekely *chaise-longue*
- Toy collection

INFORMATION

- ✚ G5
- ✉ 107 rue de Rivoli 75001
- ☎ 01 44 55 57 50
- 🕐 Wed–Sat 12:30–6; Sun noon–6
- Ⓜ Palais-Royal/Musée du Louvre
- 🚌 21, 27, 39, 48, 67, 69, 72, 81
- ♿ Excellent
- 💲 Moderate
- ↔ Musée du Louvre (➤ 35)

This uncrowded museum charms you with its discreet, old-fashioned atmosphere and idiosyncratic collections. These may not necessarily be valuable, but they offer a clear view of developments in interior design and decoration.

The collection Tucked away in the northwest wing of the Louvre, this rather oddly arranged museum houses five floors of predominantly French furniture, furnishings and *objets d'art* from the Middle Ages through rococo to the present. It was founded early this century by an association of designers whose aim was to collect and exhibit "beauty in function," and it certainly lives up to its role. Subsequent donations have greatly enriched the collection, including the contents of the former Musée de la Publicité, thus adding graphic arts to the list. Extensive renovation is currently underway, closing some sections until 1999.

What to see The museum is arranged chronologically. The ground floor is devoted to a fascinating collection of 20th-century design, ranging from Le Corbusier to Nikki de St Phalle and Philippe Starck, with superb rooms devoted to art nouveau and art deco as well as temporary exhibitions. Do not miss the excellent specialist bookstore and small gift-shop at the entrance. The upper floors display medieval and Renaissance pieces, with better coverage of Louis XIII, Louis XIV, Louis XV, Empire, Restoration, Louis Philippe, and Second Empire furnishings, some of which are arranged in reconstructed décors. On the fourth floor a changing exhibition displays toys throughout the centuries beside an outstanding collection of dolls. Top-floor collections of wallpaper, glass, and graphic arts can be viewed only by appointment.

Top: Jeanne Lanvin's bedroom by A.A. Rateau (1920–1922)

MUSÉE DU LOUVRE

Nocturnal lighting transforms the Louvre's glass pyramid entrance into a gigantic cut diamond—just a foretaste of the treasures contained within. It is hard to ignore the state-of-the-art renovation, but that is just the icing on the cake.

The world's largest museum Few visitors bypass this palatial museum, but definitions of personal interest need to be made beforehand as mere wandering could become a lifetime's occupation. Since 1981 the Louvre has been undergoing a radical transformation which crowns six centuries of eventful existence and which will be completed in 1997. Originally a medieval castle, it first took shape as an art gallery under François I, eager to display his Italian loot. Catherine de Médicis extended it into a palace in 1578. After escaping the excesses of the Revolutionary mob, in 1793 it became a people's museum and was later enlarged by Napoleon I, who also greatly enriched its collection.

Mona Lisa,
Leonardo da Vinci

Art fortress The vast collection of some 30,000 exhibits is arranged on three floors of three wings: Sully (east), Richelieu (north), and Denon (south), while beneath the elegant Cour Carrée lie the keep and dungeons of the original medieval fortress. Do not miss the two spectacular skylit halls flanking the passageway from Palais-Royal, which display monumental French sculptures, nor the tasteful shops in the central marble hall.

HIGHLIGHTS

- Palace of Khorsabad
- Egyptian scribe
- Glass pyramid entrance, designed by I. M. Pei
- *Bataille de San Romano*, Uccello
- *Mona Lisa*, Leonardo da Vinci
- *La Dentellière*, Vermeer
- *Le Radeau de la Méduse*, Géricault
- *Vénus de Milo*
- *Gabrielle d'Estrées et Une des ses Soeurs*, Ecole de Fontainebleau
- Cour Carrée at night

INFORMATION

- 🔲 G5
- ✉ 99 rue de Rivoli 75001
- ☎ 01 40 20 53 17. Recorded information: 01 40 20 51 51. Auditorium: 01 40 20 51 86
- 🕐 Thu–Sun 9–6; Mon and Wed 9AM–10PM
- 🍴 Wide selection of restaurants and cafes
- Ⓜ Palais-Royal/Musée du Louvre
- 🚌 21, 27, 39, 48,67, 68, 69, 72, 75, 76, 81, 95
- ♿ Excellent
- 💰 Very expensive until 3PM, moderate after 3PM and Sun
- ↔ Musée des Arts Décoratifs (➤ 34), Musée d'Orsay (➤ 31)
- ❓ Audio and digital tours; regular lectures, films, concerts in auditorium

13

GALERIES VIVIENNE & COLBERT

HIGHLIGHTS

- Mosaic floor
- Bronze statue
- Staircase at 13 Galerie Vivienne
- Clock
- Bookstore
- Gaultier's shop

DID YOU KNOW?

- Explorer Bougainville lived here
- Revolutionary Simón Bolívar lived here
- Crook-turned-cop Vidocq lived here in the 1840s

INFORMATION

- ✚ G5
- ✉ Galerie Vivienne & Galerie Colbert 75002
- 🕐 Gate at 5 rue de la Banque is permanently open
- 🍴 A Priori Thé (➤ 72), Le Grand Colbert (➤ 71)
- 🚇 Bourse, Palais-Royal/Musée du Louvre
- 🚌 29
- ♿ Good
- 👆 Free
- ↔ Jardin du Palais-Royal (➤ 59)

The mosaic floor (top) and the bronze statue (right) in the Galerie Vivienne

These connecting 19th-century passages, with their original mosaic floors and neo-classical decoration, are a perfect place for people-watching, and they offer a complete contrast to the fashionable buzz of neighboring streets.

Shopping arcades Between the late 18th and early 19th centuries the Right Bank included a network of 140 covered passageways—the fashionable shopping malls of the time. Today there are fewer than 30, of which the Galeries Vivienne and Colbert are perhaps the best known, strategically squeezed in between the Bibliothèque Nationale and the Place des Victoires. Bookworms and fashion-victims cross paths in this elegant, skylit setting lined with potted palms, where there is also the occasional fashion show. It is perfect for a rainy day browse.

Hive of interest The Galerie Vivienne (1823) opens on to three different streets, while the parallel Galerie Colbert (1826) has its own entrances. Colbert is now an annex of the Bibliothèque Nationale, and regular exhibitions (prints, photos, theater accessories) and concerts are held in its galleries and auditorium. Galerie Vivienne is commercial in spirit: this is where you can track down Jean-Paul Gaultier's eccentric shop, designer watches, antiquarian or rare artists' books, contemporary design, fine wines, intriguing toys, or simply sit sipping exotic tea beneath the skylight, watching the world go by.

Jardin du Luxembourg

Despite the crowds, these gardens are serene in all weather and are perfect epitomes of French landscaping. Their occupants present an idealized image of an unhurried Parisian existence far from the daily truth of noise and traffic.

Layout Radiating from the large octagonal pond in front of the Palais du Luxembourg (now the Senate) are terraces, paths, and a wide tree-lined alley that leads down to the Observatory crossroads. Natural attractions include shady chestnut trees, potted orange and palm trees, lawns, and even an experimental fruit garden and orchard, while fountains, tennis courts, bee-hives, a puppet theater, and children's play-grounds offer other distractions. Statues of the queens of France, artists, and writers are dotted about the terraces and avenues.

Park activities All year round joggers work off their *foie gras* on the circumference, and in sum-mer sunbathers and bookworms settle into park chairs, card- and chess-playing retirees claim the shade in front of the palace, bands tune up at the bandstand near the Boulevard Saint-Michel entrance, and children burn off energy on swings and donkeys.

History The Palais du Luxembourg and surrounding garden were originally commis-sioned by Marie de Médicis, wife of Henri IV, in 1615, and designed to resemble her Florentine childhood home. The Allée de l'Observatoire and the English-style garden were added in the early 19th century. A petition signed by 12,000 Parisians luckily saved the garden from Haussmann's urban ambitions, and since then its formal charms have inspired countless literary and celluloid tributes.

HIGHLIGHTS

- Médicis fountain
- Cyclops, Acis, and Galateus sculptures
- Bandstand
- Statue of Delacroix
- Orange-tree conservatory
- Experimental fruit-garden
- Beekeeping school
- Statues of queens of France

DID YOU KNOW?

- Isadora Duncan danced here
- Ernest Hemingway claimed to capture pigeons here for his supper

INFORMATION

- ✚ G7
- ✉ 15 rue de Vaugirard 75006
- ☎ Senate: 01 42 34 20 00
- 🕐 Apr–Oct daily 7:30AM–9:30PM. Nov–Mar daily 8.15–5 (times may vary slightly)
- 🍴 Open-air cafés, kiosk restaurant
- Ⓜ Luxembourg
- 🚌 21, 27, 38, 58, 82, 84, 85, 89
- 🚆 RER Line B Luxembourg
- ♿ Very good
- 💶 Free
- ↔ Eglise de Saint-Sulpice (► 52)

MUSÉE DE CLUNY

HIGHLIGHTS

- *La Dame à la Licorne* tapestries
- Gold altar frontal
- *Pilier des Nautes*
- Heads from Notre-Dame
- Visigoth votive crown
- Italian processional cross
- Statue of Adam
- Stained glass
- Averbode altarpiece
- Abbot's Chapel

INFORMATION

- H7
- 6 Place Paul-Painlevé 75006
- 01 53 73 78 00
- Wed–Mon 9:15–5:45
- Cluny-La Sorbonne
- 21, 27, 38, 63, 85, 86, 87, 96
- Moderate
- Sainte-Chapelle (➤ 39)
- Guided tours of vaults: Wed, Sat, Sun 2PM. Tours of collection at 3:30PM

Take a deep breath outside the Musée de Cluny (officially the Musée National du Moyen-Age/Thermes de Cluny) and prepare to enter a time warp in which the days of the troubadours and courtly love are re-created in its paneled rooms.

Baths The late 2nd-century Gallo-Roman baths adjoining the Hôtel de Cluny are composed of three stone chambers: the Caldarium (steam bath), the Tepidarium (tepid bath), and the Frigidarium (cold bath), with ruins of the former gymnasium visible on the Boulevard Saint-Germain side. Important Roman stonework is exhibited in the niches, while Room VIII houses 21 mutilated heads from Notre-Dame. Recent excavations have also opened up a labyrinth of Roman vaults which can be toured with a guide.

Treasures The Gothic turreted mansion was built in 1500 by the abbot Jacques d'Amboise and is one of France's finest examples of domestic architecture of this period. Some 23,000 objects compose the collection, much of which was gathered by the 19th-century medievalist and collector, Alexandre du Sommerard. Perhaps the most famous piece is the beautiful *La Dame à la Licorne* tapestry, woven in the late 15th century. Six enigmatic panels depict a woman, a lion, and a unicorn, animals, flowers, and birds, all exquisitely worked. Costumes, accessories, textiles, and tapestries are of Byzantine, Coptic, or European origin, while the gold- and metalwork room houses some outstanding pieces of Gallic, Barbarian, Merovingian, and Visigoth artistry. Stained glass, table games, ceramics, wood carvings, illuminated manuscripts and Books of Hours, altarpieces, and religious statuary complete this exceptional and very manageable display.

Top: A mon Seul Désir, *one of the* La Dame à la Licorne *tapestries*

SAINTE-CHAPELLE

Sainte-Chapelle's 246-foot spire soaring towards the heavens is in itself an extraordinary expression of faith, but inside this is surpassed by the glowing intensity of the magnificent stained-glass windows reaching up to a star-studded roof.

Masterpiece One of Paris's oldest and most significant monuments stands within the precincts of the Palais de Justice. The chapel was built by Louis IX (later canonized) to house relics he had acquired at exorbitant cost during the crusades, and which included what was reputed to be the Crown of Thorns, as well as fragments of the

Cross and drops of Christ's blood (now kept in Notre-Dame). Pierre de Montreuil masterminded this delicate Gothic construction, bypassing the use of flying buttresses, incorporating a lower chapel for palace servants and installing 6,650 square feet of stained glass above. Completed in 1248 in record time, it served as Louis IX's private chapel with discreet access from what was then the royal palace.

Apocalypse No fewer than 1,134 biblical scenes are illustrated in the 16 windows, starting with Genesis and finishing with the Apocalypse (the central rose window). To follow the narrative chronologically, read from left to right and bottom to top, row by row. The statues of the Apostles against the pillars are mostly copies—the damaged originals are at the Musée de Cluny.

HIGHLIGHTS

- Rose window
- Oratory
- 19th-century restoration
- Tombs of canons
- Stained glass depiction of Christ's Passion
- St. Louis himself in the 15th window

INFORMATION

- ✛ H6
- ✉ 4 Boulevard du Palais 75001
- ☎ 01 53 73 78 51
- 🕐 Oct–Mar daily 10–4:30. Apr–Sep daily 9:30–6
- Ⓜ Cité, Saint-Michel
- 🚌 21, 38, 85, 96
- 🚇 RER Line B, Saint-Michel
- ♿ Moderate
- ↔ Musée de Cluny (➤ 38)

Top: the stained-glass windows of the upper chapel

39

CONCIERGERIE

HIGHLIGHTS

- Public clock
- Sculptures
- Barber's cell
- Tour Bonbec

DID YOU KNOW?

- 288 prisoners were massacred here in 1792
- 4,164 citizens were held here during the Terror
- Comte d'Armagnac was assassinated here
- 22 left-wing Girondins were held in one room
- Robespierre spent only one night here before his execution
- There were three types of cell according to prisoners' means

INFORMATION

- ✚ H6
- ✉ 1 Quai de l'Horloge 75001
- ☎ 01 53 73 78 50
- ◷ Oct–Mar daily 10–4:30. Apr–Sep daily 9:30–6
- Ⓜ Cité, Châtelet
- 🚌 21, 38, 85, 96
- ♿ Moderate
- ↔ Sainte-Chapelle (▶ 39)
- ❓ Guided tours: daily 11AM and 3PM

The ghosts of the victims of the guillotine must surely haunt this stark and gloomy place, which served as a prison and torture chamber for over five centuries, and which remains full of macabre mementos of its grisly past.

Gloom Rising over the Seine in menacing splendor, the turreted Conciergerie was built in 1299–1313 originally to house Philippe-le-Bel's caretaker (*concierge*) and palace guards, and with Sainte-Chapelle it formed part of a royal complex on the Ile de la Cité. The square, corner tower displays Paris's first public clock, an ornate masterpiece constructed in 1370 and restored along with the rest of the Gothic interior in the 19th century. Access to the Conciergerie is through the Salle des Gardes, a vaulted stone chamber now plunged into shadow by the embankment outside, which in turn opens on to the vast but equally gloomy Salle des Gens d'Armes. This is thought to be Europe's oldest-surviving medieval hall, and is where members of the royal household ate their meals. From here, a curious spiral staircase leads to the original kitchens.

Victims From 1391 until 1914 the building functioned as a prison and torture chamber, its reputation striking terror into the hearts of thousands. A network of cells, both shared and private, lines the corridor (the rue de Paris) leading to the Galerie des Prisonniers, where lawyers, prisoners, and visitors once mingled. A staircase leads up to rooms relating the Conciergerie's bloody history (including a list of the guillotine's 2,278 victims); back downstairs are re-creations of the Chapelle des Girondins, and the cells occupied by Marie-Antoinette, Danton and Robespierre.

Top: Salle des Gens d'Armes

CENTRE GEORGES POMPIDOU

Late opening hours make an exhibition visit possible between an aperitif and dinner in this still-controversial cultural center. You can take your pick between the genesis of modernism, an art film, or a drama performance.

High-tech culture More than a mere landmark in the extensive face-lift that Paris has undergone in the last 20 years, the high-tech Centre Pompidou (commonly known as Beaubourg) is a hive of constantly changing cultural activity. Contemporary art, architecture, design, photography, theater, cinema, and dance are all represented, while the lofty structure itself offers exceptional views over

central Paris. Take the transparent escalator tubes for a bird's-eye view of the piazza below, where musicians, street artists, and portraitists ply their trades to the teeming crowds.

Face-lift From October 1997 to the eve of the millennium in December 1999, the center will undergo major restructuring

The fountain in nearby Place Igor Stravinsky

and refurbishing. Radically reduced exhibition space and access to the top-floor panoramas remain, but otherwise the center is essentially closed. On reopening in the year 2000, the layout will have gained in logic but perhaps lost in atmosphere. In the meantime, visit the reopened Atelier Brancusi on the piazza, or spend francs at the museum store housed in the temporary tepee in front of the center.

HIGHLIGHTS

- Design by Richard Rogers, Renzo Piano, and Gianfranco Franchini
- Stravinsky fountain
- *The Deep*, Jackson Pollock
- *Phoque*, Brancusi
- *Le Magasin*, Ben
- *Bleu II*, Miró
- *Infiltration homogène*, Joseph Beuys
- Gouache cut-outs, Matisse
- *Improvisations*, Kandinsky
- Electronic countdown to the year 2000

INFORMATION

H5/6

Rue Rambuteau 75004

01 44 78 12 33.
Information on daily events:
01 42 77 11 12

Mon, Wed–Fri noon–10; Sat–Sun 10–10

Mediocre cafeteria with a view

Rambuteau, Hôtel de Ville

38, 47

RER Line A B, Châtelet-Les Halles

Excellent

Very expensive; free on Sun 10–2

Musée National des Techniques (▶ 51)

Guided and audio tours to Musée National d'Art Moderne; frequent lectures, concerts, parallel activities, Atelier des Enfants

MARCHÉ AUX PUCES DE SAINT-OUEN

HIGHLIGHTS

- Marché Serpette: antiques, art deco, jewelry
- Marché Paul Bert: antiques, quality bric-a-brac
- Marché Jules Vallè: bric-a-brac, furniture, prints
- Marché Biron: reproduction furniture, *objets d'art*
- Marché Vernaison: antiques
- Marché Cambo: paintings, furniture
- Marché Malik: secondhand clothes, accessories, ethnic goods

INFORMATION

- ✚ G1
- ✉ Porte de Clignancourt
- 🕐 Sat–Mon 7:30–5
- 🍴 Cafés and restaurants on rue des Rosiers
- Ⓜ Porte de Clignancourt, Porte de Saint-Ouen
- 🚌 56, 60, 81, 95
- ♿ Good
- 🎟 Free
- ↔ Sacré-Coeur (➤ 33)
- ❓ Beware of pickpockets

A Sunday pastime favored by many locals is to look for bargains at the city's flea markets, of which the crème de la crème *is still this one. Nowhere else will you find such a fascinating cross-section of Parisian society.*

Duck and banter The approach from the métro to this sprawling 75-acre market is uninspiring as it entails bypassing household goods, jeans, and shoe stands before ducking under the *périphérique* overpass and finally entering the fray. Persevere and you may discover an antique gem, a fake, or a secondhand pilot's jacket. Everything and anything is displayed here but all commerce is carried on in the true bantering style of the *faubourgs*, a habit that dates from the late 19th century when the first junkmen moved in to offer their wares for sale.

Bargain Registered dealers are divided into seven official markets, which interconnect through passageways bustling with crowds. Along the fringes are countless hopefuls who set up temporary stands to sell a mind-boggling range of goods from obsolete kitchenware to old jukeboxes and cheap junk. Although unashamedly a tourist trap, there is something for everyone here, but do go early—trading starts at 7:30AM. Bargaining is obligatory and prices are directly related to the weather: high on sunny, crowded days and low under cold, wet skies. Stop for lunch in one of the animated bistros along the rue des Rosiers—try the garden setting of Chez la Mère Marie at No. 82 (☎ 01 40 11 90 48). On weekends as many as 150,000 bargain-hunters, tourists, and dealers can cram the passageways—avoid Sunday afternoons in particular, when the throng reaches claustrophobic proportions and pickpockets abound.

NOTRE-DAME

"Spectacular" is the word that springs to mind when describing Paris's most extra-ordinary monument, with its 295-foot spire and some of the world's best-known flying buttresses. One of the best views of the cathedral is from the quais to the east.

Evolution Construction started on this labor of love and faith in 1163 but it was not finished until 1345, making it transitional in style between Romanesque and Gothic. Since then the cathedral has suffered from pollution, politics, aesthetic trends, and religious change. Louis XV declared stained glass outmoded and replaced most of the rose windows with clear glass (the stained glass was later restored), Revolutionary anticlericalism toppled countless statues, and the spire was amputated in 1787. Not least, Viollet-le-Duc, the fervent 19th-century medievalist architect, was let loose on its restoration and made radical alterations.

Interior grandeur The gloomy stone interior contains numerous chapels, tombs, and statues, as well as the sacristy (south side of choir) where the treasure of Notre-Dame is kept. Climb the towers—386 steps—for fantastic views and a closeup of the gargoyles. Look closely at the three asymmetrical sculpted portals on the façade: these once served as a Bible for illiterate worshippers. Finally, walk round the cathedral for a view of its extravagant flying buttresses.

HIGHLIGHTS

- South rose window
- Porte Rouge
- Portail du Cloître
- Sculptures of Ste. Anne
- Treasure of Notre-Dame
- Emmanuel bell
- 1730 organ
- *Pietà*, Nicolas Coustou
- Statue of Notre-Dame de Paris
- Choir stalls

INFORMATION

- ✠ H6
- ✉ Place du Parvis Notre-Dame 75004
- ☎ 01 42 34 56 10. Crypt: 01 43 29 83 51
- ◷ Cathedral: daily 8–7. Tower and crypt: Oct–Mar daily 10–4:30. Apr–Sep daily 10–5:30
- Ⓜ Cité, Saint-Michel
- 🚌 24, 47
- 🚊 RER Lines B and C, Saint-Michel
- ♿ Good
- 🎟 Cathedral: free. Tower and crypt: moderate
- ↔ Musée de Cluny (➤ 38), Ile Saint-Louis (➤ 44)
- 🎵 Organ recitals at 5:30PM on Sun

The southern aspect of Notre-Dame, showing the south rose window (detail above)

43

ILE SAINT-LOUIS

HIGHLIGHTS

- Eglise Saint-Louis-en-l'Isle
- Arch of Hôtel de Bretonvilliers
- Hôtel Lambert
- Camille Claudel's home and studio
- Square Barye
- Brasserie de l'Ile
- Pont Marie
- High-water mark, 1 Quai d'Anjou
- Helena Rubinstein's home

INFORMATION

- H/J6/7
- Sunny terrace of La Brasserie de l'Ile
- Pont Marie, Sully Morland
- 67, 86, 87
- Good
- Notre-Dame (➤ 43)

Floating mid-Seine is this fascinating residential island, a living museum of 17th-century architecture and also a popular tourist haunt. Join the crowds and spot an illustrious resident, but above all indulge in the island's own ice cream.

History Once a marshy swamp, the Ile Saint-Louis was transformed into an elegant residential area in the 17th century, when it was joined to the

Courtyard, Quai de Bourbon

Ile de la Cité. Today, six bridges link it to the Rive Droite and the Rive Gauche, but nevertheless it still maintains a spirit of its own, and residents openly boast that its food stores are unsurpassable. Cutting across it lengthwise is rue Saint-Louis-en-l'Ile, lined with upscale groceries, arts and craft shops, and restaurants, and also home to the Eglise Saint-Louis-en-l'Isle, begun by Le Vau in 1664. The side streets here are mainly residential.

Hashish The Quai d'Anjou, on the northeast side, has a rich past. Former residents include the architect himself, Le Vau, at No. 3, Honoré Daumier (No. 9), Baudelaire, and Théophile Gautier who, at No. 17, animated his Club des Haschichins. Commemorative plaques to the famous pepper the façades of the island's harmonious townhouses, and the riverside paths offer quintessential Parisian views, romantic trysts, and summer sunbathing. Before leaving, make sure you try a Berthillon ice cream, reputedly the best in the world!

INSTITUT DU MONDE ARABE

It is difficult to miss this gleaming, ultra-contemporary building as you cross the Seine. Although some may find it limited, the museum's collection nevertheless offers a sleekly presented introduction to the brilliance of Islamic civilization.

Arab inspiration Clean lines, aluminum walls, and glass are the hallmarks of Jean Nouvel's design for the Arab Institute, which was inaugurated in 1980 to foster cultural exchange between Islamic countries and the West. Innovative features include high-speed transparent elevators, a system of high-tech metal screens on the south elevation which filter light entering the institute and which were inspired by the *musharabia* (carved wooden screens) on traditional Arab buildings, and an enclosed courtyard achieved by splitting the building in two. The institute's facilities comprise a museum, library, exhibition halls, lecture and concert halls, and an elegant rooftop café boasting spectacular panoramas across the Seine.

Museum First take the elevator to the 9th floor for sweeping views across the Ile Saint-Louis and northeastern Paris, then head down to the museum on the 7th floor. Here, finely crafted metalwork, ceramics, textiles, carpets, and calligraphy reflect the exceptional talents of Islamic civilization, although the collection remains small in relation to its ambitious setting. Temporary exhibitions are often of a high quality and cover both historical and contemporary themes in arts, crafts, and photography. There is an audiovisual center in the basement with thousands of slides, photographs, films, and sound recordings, and current news broadcasts from all over the Arab world are also available for viewing.

HIGHLIGHTS

- Light screens
- Astrolabes in museum
- Statue of Amma'alay
- Head of sun god
- Rope and palm-fiber sandal
- Sultan Selim III's Koran
- Miniature of Emperor Aurengzeb
- Indian glass vase
- Egyptian child's tunic

INFORMATION

- J7
- 1 rue des Fossés Saint-Bernard 75005
- 01 40 51 38 38
- Tue–Sun 10–6
- Convivial snack bar open until midnight; tea room
- Jussieu, Cardinal Lemoine
- 24, 63, 67, 86, 87, 89
- Excellent
- Moderate
- Ile Saint-Louis (➤ 44), Arènes de Lutèce (➤ 59)
- Occasional Arab music, films, and plays

MUSÉE CARNAVALET

INFORMATION

- ✚ J6
- ✉ 23 rue de Sévigné 75003
- ☎ 01 42 72 21 13
- ⏰ Tue–Sat 10–5:40
- Ⓜ Saint-Paul
- 🚌 29, 96
- ♿ Excellent
- 💷 Moderate
- ↔ Place des Vosges (➤ 47), Musée Picasso (➤ 51)
- ❓ Photography exhibitions

There is no better museum than this to plunge you into the history of Paris, and its renovated mansion setting is hard to beat. Period rooms, artifacts, documents, paintings, and objets d'art *combine to swing you through the city's turbulent past.*

Ornamental excess This captivating collection is displayed within two adjoining 16th- and 17th-century townhouses. Entrance is through the superb courtyard of the Hôtel Carnavalet (1548), once home of the celebrated writer Madame de Sévigné. Here attention focusses on the Roman period, the Middle Ages, the Renaissance, and the heights of decorative excess reached under Louis XIV, Louis XV, and Louis XVI. Some of the richly painted and sculpted interiors are original to the building; others, such as the wood paneling from the Hôtel Colbert de Villacerf and Brunetti's *trompe-l'oeil* staircase paintings, have been brought in.

Revolution to the present Next door, the well-renovated Hôtel Le Peletier de Saint-Fargeau (1690) exhibits some remarkable objects from the Revolution—a period when anything and everything was emblazoned with slogans—and continues with Napoleon I's reign, the Restoration, the Second Empire, the Commune, and finally the Belle Epoque. Illustrious figures such as Robespierre and Madame Le Récamier come to life within their chronological context. The collection ends in the early 20th century with some remarkable reconstructions of interiors, and paintings by Utrillo, Signac, Marquet, and Foujita.

PLACE DES VOSGES

Paris's best-preserved square connects the quarters of the Marais and the Bastille. Visitors always marvel at its architectural unity and love to stroll under its arcades, now animated by outdoor restaurants and window-shoppers.

Place Royale Ever since the square was inaugurated in 1612 with a spectacular fireworks display, countless luminaries have chosen to live in the red-brick houses overlooking the central garden of plane trees. Before that, the square was the site of a royal palace, the Palais des Tournelles (1407), which was later abandoned and demolished by Catherine de Médicis in 1559 when her husband Henri II died in a tournament. The arcaded façades were commissioned by the enlightened Henri IV, who incorporated two royal pavilions at the center of the north and south sides of the square and named it "Place Royale."

Celebrities After the Revolution the square was renamed Place des Vosges in honor of the first French district to pay its new taxes. The first example of planned development in the history of Paris, these 36 townhouses (nine on each side and still intact after four centuries) with their steep-pitched roofs surround a formal garden laid out with gravel paths and fountains. The elegant symmetry of the houses has always attracted a string of celebrities. Princesses, official mistresses, Cardinal Richelieu, the Duc de Sully, Victor Hugo (his house is now a museum) and Théophile Gautier, and more recently the late painter Francis Bacon, Beaubourg's architect Richard Rogers, and former minister of culture, Jack Lang, have all lived here. Upscale shops and chic art galleries, with prices to match and perfect for window-gazing, line its arcades.

HIGHLIGHTS

- Pavillon du Roi
- Statue of Louis XIII
- Hôtel de Coulanges
- No. 6, Maison Victor Hugo
- No. 21, residence of Cardinal Richelieu
- Archaeological finds at No. 18
- Door knockers
- *Trompe-l'oeil* bricks
- Auvergne sausages at Ma Bourgogne restaurant

INFORMATION

- ✚ J6
- ✉ Place des Vosges 75004
- 🍴 Ma Bourgogne (➤ 73)
- 🚇 Bastille, Chemin Vert, Saint-Paul
- 🚌 29, 96
- ♿ Good
- 🎫 Free
- ↔ Hôtel de Sully (➤ 17), Musée Carnavalet (➤ 46)

47

CIMETIÈRE DU PÈRE LACHAISE

HIGHLIGHTS

- Oscar Wilde's tomb
- Edith Piaf's tomb
- Chopin's tomb
- Marcel Proust's tomb
- Mur des Fédérés
- Delacroix's tomb
- Tomb of Victor Hugo's family
- Baron Haussmann's tomb
- Molière's tomb
- Jim Morrison's tomb

INFORMATION

- ✚ L/M5/6
- ✉ Boulevard de Ménilmontant 75020
- ☎ 01 43 70 70 33
- 🕐 Oct–Mar daily 8–5:30. Apr–Sep Mon–Fri 8–6; Sat 8:30–5:30/6; Sun 9–5:30/6
- Ⓜ Père Lachaise
- 🚌 61, 69
- ♿ Excellent
- 🎫 Free

If you think cemeteries are lugubrious then a visit to Père Lachaise might change your mind. A plethora of tomb designs, shady trees, and twisting paths combine to create a peaceful setting that has become a popular park.

Pilgrimage This landscaped hillside, up in the *faubourgs* of Ménilmontant, is now a favorite haunt for rock fans, Piaf fans, and lovers of poetry, literature, music, and history. Since its creation in 1803 this vast cemetery has seen hundreds of the famous and illustrious buried within its precincts, so that a walk around its labyrinthine expanse presents a microcosm of French sociocultural history. Pick up a plan at the entrance or the kiosk by the métro, then set off on this Parisian path of the Holy Grail to track down your heroes.

Incumbents The cemetery was created in 1803 on land once owned by Louis XIV's confessor, Father La Chaise. It was the site of the Communards' tragic last stand in 1871, when the 147 survivors of a nightlong fight met their bloody end in front of a government firing-squad and were thrown into a communal grave, now commemorated by the Mur des Fédérés in the eastern corner. A somber reminder of the victims of World War II are the memorials to those who died in the Nazi concentration camps. Paths meander past striking funerary monuments and the graves of such well-known figures as the star-crossed medieval lovers Abélard and Héloïse, painters Delacroix and Modigliani, actress Sarah Bernhardt, composers Poulenc and Bizet, and writers Balzac and Colette. Crowds of rock fans throng round the tomb of Jim Morrison, singer with The Doors, whose death in Paris in 1971 is still a mystery.

PARIS's
best

49

MUSEUMS & GALLERIES

Other museums

If you are hooked on the intimate atmosphere of one-man museums, then head for the former home/studio of sculptor Antoine Bourdelle, recently renovated by top architect Christian de Portzamparc (⊠ 18 rue Antoine Bourdelle 75014 ⊚ Falguière). Other jewels include the Maison Victor Hugo (➤ 47), the Musée Delacroix (➤ 60), the Musée Hébert (➤ 60), and the Maison de Balzac (47 rue Raynouard 75016 ⊚ Passy).

Visit the Musée d'Art Moderne for modern and contemporary paintings and sculpture

CITÉ DES SCIENCES ET DE L'INDUSTRIE

Vast, enthralling display covering the earth, the universe, life, communications, natural resources, technology, and industry. There are temporary exhibitions, a planetarium, a children's section and a THX cinema, La Géode (➤ 58).

➕ L2 ⊠ 30 Avenue Corentin Cariou 75019 ☎ 08 36 68 29 30 ⊙ Tue–Sat 10–6; Sun 10–7 🍴 Cafés in park ⊚ Porte de la Villette 💺 Very expensive

MAISON EUROPÉENNE DE LA PHOTOGRAPHIE

Stylish new center for contemporary photography, which has permanent displays and stages dynamic temporary shows.

➕ J6 ⊠ 5–7 rue de Fourcy 75004 ☎ 01 44 78 75 00 ⊙ Wed–Sun 11AM–8PM ⊚ Saint-Paul 💺 Moderate

MUSÉE D'ART MODERNE DE LA VILLE DE PARIS

Dufy's mural *La Fée Electricité*, Matisse's *La Danse*, and a solid collection of the early moderns offer a parallel to exhibitions of contemporary avant-garde artists.

➕ D5 ⊠ 11 Avenue du Président Wilson 75016 ☎ 01 53 67 40 00 ⊙ Tue, Thu–Fri 10–5:30; Wed 10–8:30; Sat–Sun 10–7 🍴 Cafeteria ⊚ Iéna, Alma-Marceau 💺 Expensive

MUSÉE GUSTAVE MOREAU

This museum is dedicated solely to the Symbolist painter Gustave Moreau (teacher of Matisse and Rouault), and is housed in his former home/ studio. Evocative paintings, watercolors, and drawings.

🔲 G4 ✉ 14 rue de la Rochefoucauld 75009 ☎ 01 48 74 38 50
🕐 Thu–Sun 10–12:45, 2–5:15; Mon and Wed 11–5:15 🚇 Trinité
🏷 Moderate

MUSÉE NATIONAL DES ARTS AFRICAINS ET OCÉANIENS

Fascinating artifacts from the Pacific, Africa, and Maghreb, extending to Australian aboriginal art. Sculptures, textiles, jewelry, and masks. Kids love the aquariums, and the building (1931) is stunning.

🔲 M8 ✉ 293 Avenue Daumesnil 75012 ☎ 01 44 74 84 80; 01 43 46 51 61 🕐 Wed–Mon 10–12, 1:30–5:30; Sat–Sun 12:30–6
🚇 Porte Dorée 🏷 Moderate

MUSÉE NATIONAL DES TECHNIQUES

An eccentric museum where art meets science through antique clocks, glass, vintage cars, optics, and mechanical toys. Undergoing massive renovation; some parts remain closed until 1998.

🔲 J5 ✉ 292 rue Saint-Martin 75003 ☎ 01 40 27 23 31
🕐 Tue–Sun 10–5 🚇 Arts et Métiers, Réaumur-Sébastopol
🏷 Moderate

MUSÉE DU PANTHÉON BOUDDHIQUE (GUIMET)

While the magnificent Musée Guimet remains closed for major restructuring until mid-1999, visit the annex to meditate on Japanese and Chinese Buddhas.

🔲 D5 ✉ 19 Avenue d'Iéna 75116 ☎ 01 47 23 61 65
🕐 Wed–Mon 9:45–5:45 🚇 Iéna 🏷 Moderate

MUSÉE PICASSO

Massive collection of Picasso's paintings, sculptures, drawings, and ceramics in a beautifully renovated 17th-century mansion. The fixtures are by Diego Giacometti, and some of the works are by Picasso's contemporaries.

🔲 J6 ✉ Hôtel Salé, 5 rue de Thorigny 75003 ☎ 01 42 71 25 21
🕐 Wed–Mon 9:30–5:30 🚇 Chemin Vert 🚌 29 🏷 Moderate

MUSÉUM NATIONAL D'HISTOIRE NATURELLE

Spectacular displays of comparative anatomy, paleontology, and mineralogy. Interesting temporary exhibitions and botanic gardens (1635).

🔲 J8 ✉ 57 rue Cuvier 75005 ☎ 01 40 79 30 00 🕐 Wed–Mon 10–5; Thu 10–10. Entomology: 1–5 🚇 Monge, Gare d'Austerlitz
🏷 Expensive; reduced in morning

Grand Nu au Fauteuil Rouge *(1929)*, in the Picasso Museum

Musée Picasso

The contents of the Musée Picasso—no fewer than 200 paintings, 158 sculptures, and 3,000 drawings—were acquired by France in lieu of inheritance tax. The process of evaluating Picasso's vast estate was no simple task as he had the annoying habit of leaving a château once the rooms were filled with his prodigious works. Eleven years of cataloguing followed by legal wrangling with his heirs finally produced this superb selection, one-quarter of his collection.

51

PLACES OF WORSHIP

Saint-Etienne-du-Mont

Saint-Germain-des-Prés

The first church of Saint-Germain-des-Prés was erected in the 6th century in the middle of fields (*les prés*). From the 8th century the abbey was part of a Benedictine monastery but was destroyed by the Normans, after which the present church was built. The abbey was surrounded by a fortified wall and adjoined a bishop's palace, but this eventually made way for housing in the late 17th century.

See Top 25 Sights for
NOTRE-DAME ▶ 43
SACRÉ-COEUR ▶ 33
SAINTE-CHAPELLE ▶ 39

EGLISE SAINT-ETIENNE-DU-MONT
Bizarre architectural combination of Gothic, Renaissance, and classical dating from 15th century. Unique carved-wood screen arching over the nave.
✚ H7 ✉ Place Sainte-Genevieve 75005 🚇 Cardinal Lemoine

EGLISE DE SAINT-EUSTACHE
Renaissance in detail and decoration but medieval in general design. Frequent organ recitals.
✚ H5 ✉ Rue Rambuteau 75001 🚇 Les Halles

EGLISE DE SAINT-GERMAIN-DES-PRÉS
Paris's oldest abbey dates from the 10th century; it preserves 12th-century flying buttresses, an original tower, and a choir. Regular organ recitals.
✚ G6 ✉ Place Saint-Germain-des-Prés 75006
🚇 Saint-Germain-des-Prés

EGLISE DE SAINT-MERRI
Superb example of Flamboyant Gothic though not completed until 1612. Renaissance stained glass, murals, impressive organ loft, and Paris's oldest church bell (1331). Concerts are held regularly.
✚ H6 ✉ 78 rue Saint-Martin 75003 🚇 Hôtel de Ville

EGLISE DE SAINT-SÉVERIN
Rebuilt in the 13th–16th centuries on the site of a 12th-century oratory. Inside is an impressive double ambulatory, palm-tree vaulting, and the Chapelle Mansart. Some stained glass originated at Saint-Germain-des-Prés (late 14th century).
✚ H6 ✉ 1 rue des Prêtres Saint-Séverin 75005 🚇 Saint-Michel

EGLISE DE SAINT-SULPICE
Construction started in 1646 and ended 134 years later, producing asymmetrical towers and very mixed styles. Note Delacroix's murals in the first chapel on the right, France's largest organ, and statues by Bouchardon.
✚ G7 ✉ Place Saint-Sulpice 75006 🕐 7:30–7:30
🚇 Saint-Sulpice

LA MOSQUÉE
This startling Moorish construction (1926) has a richly decorated interior, patio, and arcaded garden. Relax in the hammam (see panel ▶ 85) or sip mint tea.
✚ J8 ✉ Place du Puits-de-l'Ermite 75005 ☎ 01 45 35 97 33
🕐 Guided tours: 9–12, 2–6. Closed Fri 🍴 Tea room 🚇 Monge
💰 Inexpensive

CULT CAFÉS

LES DEUX MAGOTS
Some 25 whiskey brands, a good concentration of tourists, and the literary shades of Mallarmé, André Breton, and Hemingway. Strategic spot for street artists.
🞦 G6 ✉ 6 Place Saint-Germain-des-Prés 75006
☎ 01 45 48 55 25
🕐 Daily 7:30AM–2AM
🚇 Saint-Germain-des-Prés

Les Deux Magots, in Place Saint-Germain-des-Prés

CAFÉ BEAUBOURG
Opposite Beaubourg, and a favorite with artists, critics, and book-reading poseurs. Discreet tables in spacious setting designed by Christian de Portzamparc. A good winter retreat.
🞦 H6 ✉ 100 rue Saint-Martin 75004 ☎ 01 48 87 89 98
🕐 Daily 8AM–2AM 🚇 Hôtel de Ville

LA CLOSERIE DES LILAS
Hot spot of history's makers and shakers, including Lenin, Trotsky, Verlaine, and James Joyce.
🞦 G8 ✉ 171 Boulevard du Montparnasse 75006 ☎ 01 43 26 70 50 🕐 Daily 11AM–1:30AM 🚇 Vavin, Raspail

CAFÉ DE FLORE
Haunted by ghosts of existentialists Sartre and De Beauvoir, who held court here during the Occupation. Wildly overpriced but great for people-watching.
🞦 G6 ✉ 172 Boulevard Saint-Germain ☎ 01 45 48 55 26
🕐 Daily 7:45AM–1:30AM 🚇 Saint-Germain-des-Prés

CAFÉ MARLY
The latest in fashionable watering holes. Elegance is assured by the setting overlooking the Louvre pyramid, and by Olivier Gagnère's intelligent decoration.
🞦 G5 ✉ Cour Napoléon, 93 rue de Rivoli 75001 ☎ 01 49 26 06 60 🕐 Daily 8AM–2AM 🚇 Palais-Royal/Musée du Louvre

CAFÉ DE LA PAIX
Excessively mid-19th century décor designed by Charles Garnier. Extravagant setting. Touristy.
🞦 G4 ✉ 12 Boulevard des Capucines 75009 ☎ 01 40 07 30 20
🕐 Daily 10AM–1AM 🚇 Opéra

LA PALETTE
Firmly established Left Bank arty bar/café. Run with an iron glove by bearded Jean-François, not to be trifled with. Lovely tree-shaded terrace in summer.
🞦 G6 ✉ 43 rue de Seine 75006 ☎ 01 43 26 84 87 🕐 Mon–Sat 8AM–2AM. Closed Aug 🚇 Odéon.

The croissant
As you sit over your morning *café au lait* chewing a croissant, meditate on the origins of this quintessential French product. It was invented when Vienna was besieged by the Turks in 1683. A baker heard underground noises and informed the authorities, who found the enemy tunneling away into the city. The baker's reward was permission to produce pastries—so he created one in the form of the Islamic crescent.

53

20TH-CENTURY ARCHITECTURE

**See Top 25 Sights for
CENTRE GEORGES POMPIDOU ➤ 41
INSTITUT DU MONDE ARABE ➤ 45**

Grands projets

President Mitterrand was responsible for many of Paris's late-20th-century monuments. For over a decade cranes groaned as the state's *grands projets* emerged from their foundations. Intellectual criteria often came before functional considerations, and consequently not all monuments operate successfully. The Louvre renovation, topped by I. M. Pei's pyramid, is a notable exception.

The Grande Arche at La Defense

BIBLIOTHÈQUE DE FRANCE
Mitterrand's last pet *grand projet*. Dominique Perrault's symbolic design was dogged by technical and functional problems until it finally opened in early 1997.
🚇 K8 ✉ 9 Boulevard Vincent Auriol 75013 ☎ 01 53 79 53 79 🕐 Open to researchers only Ⓜ Quai de la Gare

CITÉ DE LA MUSIQUE
Finally completed in 1995 after 16 years of delays and political volte-faces, with a monumental design in white stone by Christian de Portzamparc. Houses a music school, concert hall, and museum of music.
🚇 L2 ✉ Parc de la Villette ☎ 01 44 84 45 45 🕐 Tue–Sun noon–6 🍴 Café Ⓜ Porte de Pantin

LA GRANDE ARCHE
A marble window on the world designed by Otto Von Spreckelsen and completed for the 1989 Bicentennial. Take the exterior elevator for views along the city's historical La Défense–Arc de Triomphe–Louvre axis.
🚇 Off map at A2 ✉ 1 Parvis de La Défense ☎ 01 49 07 27 57 🕐 Oct–Mar Mon–Fri 10–6. Apr–Sep Mon–Fri 10–7; Sat–Sun 9–8 Ⓜ La Défense 💰 Expensive

MAISON DU VERRE
Designed in art deco style by Pierre Chareau in 1932. Astonishing use of glass.
🚇 G6 ✉ 31 rue Saint-Guillaume 75006 Ⓜ Rue du Bac

NO. 26 RUE VAVIN
This striking, innovative building—designed by Henri Sauvage in 1925—is faced in blue and white ceramic and has stepped balconies.
🚇 G7 ✉ 26 rue Vavin 75006 Ⓜ Vavin

PORTE DAUPHINE
The best remaining example (1902) of Hector Guimard's art nouveau métro entrances, with a glass canopy and writhing sculptural structures.
🚇 C4 ✉ Avenue Bugeaud 75016 Ⓜ Porte Dauphine

RUE MALLET-STEVENS
This tiny cul-de-sac houses major symbols of "cubist" architecture (1927) by Robert Mallet-Stevens. The stark, purist lines and volumes continue at Le Corbusier's nearby Villa La Roche (1923), now a foundation.
🚇 B6 ✉ Rue Mallet-Stevens, off rue du Dr Blanche 75016 Ⓜ Jasmin

BRIDGES

PONT ALEXANDRE III
Paris's most ornate bridge, rich in gilded cupids and elaborate lamps. Built for the 1900 Exposition Universelle, and dedicated to the new Franco-Russian alliance—the foundation stone was laid by Czar Alexander III.
➕ E5 🚇 Invalides

PONT DE L'ALMA
Originally built in 1856 to commemorate victory over the Russians in the Crimean War. Replaced in 1974 but the Zouave soldier remains, one of four original statues, now acting as a high-water marker.
➕ E5 🚇 Alma-Marceau

PONT DES ARTS
The pedestrian bridge of 1804 was replaced in 1985 by an iron structure of seven steel arches crossed by resonant wooden planks. It's a favorite spot for impromptu parties and street performances.
➕ G6 🚇 Louvre-Rivoli

PONT DE BIR-HAKEIM
Paris's double-decker bridge (1903–1905) is best experienced by rattling over it in a métro. Designed by Formigé, with metal columns in art nouveau style.
➕ D6 🚇 Bir-Hakeim, Passy

PONT MARIE
Named after the Ile Saint-Louis property developer, and built in 1635. Once lined with four-story houses—some later partly destroyed by floods and others demolished in 1788.
➕ J6 🚇 Pont Marie

PONT NEUF
Built 1578–1604, Paris's oldest bridge ironically bears the name of "New Bridge." The innovative, houseless design was highly controversial at the time. In 1985 it was "wrapped" by site-artist Christo.
➕ G/H6 🚇 Pont Neuf

PONT ROYAL
Five classical arches join the Tuileries with the Faubourg Saint-Germain area. Built in 1689 by Gabriel to Mansart's design, the bridge was once used for major Parisian festivities and fireworks.
➕ G6 🚇 Palais-Royal/Musée du Louvre

36 bridges
The Paris motto *"Fluctuat nec mergitur"* ("It floats but it never sinks") did not always hold true. For centuries there were only two bridges, which linked the Ile de la Cité north and south. Subsequent wooden bridges sank without trace after floods, fires, or rivercraft collisions, so the construction of the stone Pont Neuf marked a real advance. The city's 36th bridge, Pont Charles de Gaulle, now spans the Seine between the Bibliothèque de France and Bercy.

Pont Alexandre III

GREEN SPACES

Parc Monceau

Parc de Bagatelle

On the west side of the Bois de Boulogne is the Parc de Bagatelle. Its mini-château, built in 1775, was sold in 1870 to Englishman Richard Wallace, who added further pavilions and terraces. About 700 varieties of roses bloom here and its open-air restaurant offers a romantic, summer-evening setting (see panel ➤ 66).

Jardin des Serres d'Auteuil

Off the tourist beat, and with striking late-19th century tropical greenhouses. The terrace wall is adorned with sculpted masks from Rodin's studio (⊞ A7 ✉ 3 Avenue de la Porte d'Auteuil 75016 ☎ 01 40 71 74 00 🕐 Daily 10–5 🚇 Porte d'Auteuil).

BOIS DE BOULOGNE
An area of 2,090 acres, 22 miles of paths, 150,000 trees and 300,000 bushes, and endless distractions from boating to clay-pigeon shooting and gastronomy.
⊞ A/B4/6 🕐 Permanently open 🍴 Cafés, restaurants 🚇 Porte Dauphine, Porte d'Auteuil

JARDIN DES TUILERIES
Laid out in 1564, later radically formalized by Le Nôtre. Now replanted to match adjoining Louvre. Maillol's statues rest in the shade of chestnut trees.
⊞ F/G5 ✉ Rue de Rivoli 75001 🕐 Daily dawn–dusk 🍴 Open-air cafés 🚇 Tuileries 🎟 Free

PARC ANDRÉ-CITROËN
A cool futurist park divided into specialist gardens, landscaped in 1980s on site of former Citroën factory.
⊞ C8 ✉ Rue Balard, rue Leblanc 75015 ☎ 01 45 57 13 35 🕐 Oct–Mar daily 9–6. Apr–Sep daily 9AM–10PM 🚇 Balard

PARC MONCEAU
Classic park planted in 1783 by Thomas Blaikie by order of the Duc d'Orléans. Picturesque *faux* ruins, statues and Ledoux's rotunda create timeless setting.
⊞ E3 ✉ Boulevard de Courcelles 75008 ☎ 01 42 27 08 64 🕐 Oct–Mar daily 7AM–8PM. Apr–Sep daily 7AM–10PM 🚇 Monceau

PARC MONTSOURIS
A Haussmann creation designed on English models, with copses and serpentine paths. Small lake with swans, waterfall, and grotto. Summer bandstand.
⊞ G10 ✉ Avenue Reille/ Boulevard Jourdan 75014 🕐 Oct–Mar daily 8:30–6. Apr–Sep daily 8:30AM–10PM 🍴 Restaurant 🚇 RER Line B Cité Universitaire 🎟 Free

VIEWS

Don't forget superlative panoramas from
CENTRE GEORGES POMPIDOU ➤ 41
LA GRANDE ARCHE ➤ 54
INSTITUT DU MONDE ARABE ➤ 45
NOTRE-DAME ➤ 43
SACRÉ-COEUR ➤ 33
TOUR EIFFEL ➤ 26

ARC DE TRIOMPHE
Situated at the hub of Haussmann's web of 12 avenues, and the ultimate symbol of Napoleon's military pretensions and might. Video projections.
🔲 D4 ✉ Place de l'Etoile 75008 ☎ 01 43 80 31 31 ⏰ Oct–Mar daily 10–6. Apr–Sep Sun–Mon 9:30–6; Tue–Sat 9:30AM–10:30PM 🚇 Charles de Gaulle-Etoile 💰 Expensive

LA GRANDE ROUE
Dizzy, whirling views of the Tuileries and Louvre from the Big Wheel at the heart of the fun fair.
🔲 G5 ✉ Rue de Rivoli 75001 ⏰ Late Jun–late Aug Sun–Fri noon–11:45; Sat noon–12:45AM 🚇 Tuileries 💰 Moderate

LA SAMARITAINE
The 10th floor at Magasin 2 offers a spectacular close-up on the city's Left Bank monuments. Lunch in the open air on the 9th floor or dine in newly designed splendor at the 5th-floor restaurant, Toupary (☎ 01 40 41 29 29 ⏰ Mon–Sat 8PM–1AM).
🔲 H6 ✉ Rue de la Monnaie 75001 ☎ 01 40 41 20 20 ⏰ Easter–Oct Mon–Wed, Fri–Sat 9:30–7; Thu 9:30AM–10PM 🍴 Cafeteria, restaurant 🚇 Pont Neuf 💰 Free

SQUARE DU VERT GALANT
Quintessential river-level view of bridges and the Louvre, shaded by willows and stunning at sunset.
🔲 G6 ✉ Place du Pont-Neuf 75001 ⏰ Oct–Mar daily 9–5:30. Apr–Sep daily 9AM–10PM 🚇 Pont Neuf

TOUR MONTPARNASSE
The 59th floor of this 686-foot modern tower in Montparnasse offers sweeping vistas of the city. Films on Paris are screened on the 56th floor.
🔲 F8 ✉ 33 Avenue du Maine 75015 ☎ 01 45 38 52 56 ⏰ Oct–Mar daily 9:30AM–10:30PM. Apr–Sep daily 9:30AM–11:30PM 🍴 Bar, restaurant 🚇 Montparnasse-Bienvenue 💰 Expensive

Pollution over Paris

The promised views over Paris do not always materialize as the capital is often hidden in haze trapped by the saucerlike shape of the Ile de France. Measures taken since the mid-1970s have helped: in one decade industrial pollution was reduced by 50 percent and the replacement of coal by nuclear energy and gas further cleared the air. However, carbon-monoxide levels (from vehicle exhausts) often exceed EU norms.

The view from Tour Montparnasse

CHILDREN'S ACTIVITIES

CIRQUE ALEXIS GRÜSS
Perennial favorite, with a new high-tech circus show.
🔲 A4 ✉ Allée de la Reine Marguerite, Bois de Boulogne 75016
☎ 01 45 01 53 53 🕐 Shows on Wed, Sat, Sun and public holidays
🚇 Porte d'Orléans 💵 Very expensive

DISNEYLAND PARIS
Disney's mega resort struggles with financial problems but survives.
✉ 77777 Marne-la-Vallée ☎ 01 64 74 30 00. Recorded information:
01 60 30 60 30 🕐 10–6 🍴 Cafés, restaurants 🚇 RER Line A
Marne-la-Vallée-Chessy 💵 Very expensive

LA GÉODE
This cinema's hemispherical screen plunges viewers into the heart of the action with frequent showings of nature and science films. Nearby are Le Cinaxe, a mobile cinema, and the Cité des Sciences et de l'Industrie (► 50), with other children's activities.
🔲 L2 ✉ 26 Avenue Corentin Cariou 75019 ☎ 01 36 68 29 30
🕐 Sessions Tue–Sun 🍴 Cafés in park 🚇 Porte de la Villette
💵 Very expensive

JARDIN D'ACCLIMATATION
A specially designed section of the Bois de Boulogne with puppet theater, playground, fairground, educational museum, "enchanted river," circus, zoo, and minitrain (leaves from Porte Maillot on Wed, Sat, Sun, and public holidays).
🔲 B4 ✉ Bois de Boulogne 75016 ☎ 01 40 67 90 82 🕐 Daily
10–6 🍴 Café 🚇 Les Sablons 💵 Cheap

PARC ASTÉRIX
Some 22 miles north of Paris is this very Gallic theme park, dedicated to the comic-strip hero Astérix. Plenty of animation, rides, games, and food.
✉ 60128 Plailly ☎ 03 44 62 34 34
🕐 Apr–mid-Oct Mon–Fri 10–6;
Sat–Sun 10–10 🍴 Cafés,
restaurants 🚇 RER Line B,
Roissy-Charles de Gaulle
💵 Very expensive

Le guignol

A juvenile crowd-puller dating back to the early 19th century is the *guignol*, an open-air puppet show held in several Parisian parks. You'll find them in summer on Wednesdays, weekends, and during school vacations at parks such as the Luxembourg, Montsouris, Buttes Chaumont, Champ de Mars, and the Jardin d'Acclimatation.

La Géode

FREE ATTRACTIONS

ARÈNES DE LUTÈCE
A partly ruined Gallo-Roman amphitheater now favoured by *boules*-playing retirees. Destroyed in AD 280, it was restored in the early 1900s.
➕ H7 ✉ Rue des Arènes 75005 🕐 Oct–Mar daily 8–5:30. Apr–Sep daily 8AM–10PM 🚇 Jussieu

DROUOT RICHELIEU
Let yourself be tempted at Paris's main auction rooms. A Persian carpet, a Louis XV commode, or a bunch of cutlery may come under the hammer. Auctions start at 2PM.
➕ G4 ✉ 9 rue Drouot 75009 ☎ 01 48 00 20 20 🕐 Daily 11–6. Closed Jul–Aug 🚇 Richelieu-Drouot

JARDIN DU PALAIS-ROYAL
Elegant 18th-century arcades surround this peaceful formal garden and palace (now the Conseil d'Etat and the Ministère de la Culture), redolent of Revolutionary history. Daniel Buren's conceptual striped columns occupy the Cour d'Honneur.
➕ G5 ✉ Place du Palais-Royal 75001 🕐 Oct–Mar daily 7:30AM–8:30PM. Apr–Sep daily 7AM–11PM 🍴 Restaurants, tea room 🚇 Palais-Royal/Musée du Louvre

MÉMORIAL DE LA DÉPORTATION
In the Ile de la Cité's eastern tip is a starkly designed crypt lined with 200,000 quartz pebbles to commemorate French citizens deported by the Nazis.
➕ H6 ✉ Square de l'Ile de France 75004 🕐 Mon–Fri 8:30–5:30; Sat–Sun 9–5:30 🚇 Cité

PALAIS DE JUSTICE
Follow in the footsteps of lawyers, judges, and crooks down echoing corridors, staircases, and courtyards, and, if your French is up to it, sit in on a court case. This former royal palace took on its present function during the Revolution.
➕ H6 ✉ Boulevard du Palais 75001 ☎ 01 44 32 50 00 🕐 Mon–Fri 9–6 🚇 Cité

PAVILLON DE L'ARSENAL
This strikingly designed building houses well-conceived exhibitions on urban Paris alongside a permanent display of the city's architectural evolution.
➕ J7 ✉ 21 Boulevard Morland 75004 ☎ 01 42 76 33 97 🕐 Tue–Sat 10:30–6:30; Sun 11–7 🚇 Sully Morland

Bargain Paris
Nothing comes cheap in this city of light and the *franc fort*. Still, although gastronomy, official culture, and history cost money, browsing at the *bouquinistes* along the Seine, picnicking on the river banks, reading in the parks, exploring back streets, and spinning hours away for the cost of a coffee on a *terrasse* are some of Paris's bargains.

The Palais-Royal

INTRIGUING STREETS

Cour de Rohan

A narrow cobbled passage tucked away on the Left Bank, the Cour de Rohan connects rue Saint-André-des-Arts with Boulevard Saint-Germain and dates from 1776, though it incorporates a medieval tower. It became a hive of Revolutionary activity, with Marat printing pamphlets at No. 8, Danton installed at No. 20, and the anatomy professor Dr. Guillotin (conceptor of that "philanthropic beheading machine") at No. 9.

BOULEVARD DE ROCHECHOUART
Teeming with struggling immigrants. Impromptu markets, Tati (the palace of cheap clothes), or seedy sex-shops, and a pervasive aroma of *merguez* and fries.
✚ H3 Ⓟ Barbès-Rochechouart

RUE DU CHERCHE-MIDI
César's sculpture on the rue de Sèvres crossroads marks out this typical Left Bank street, home to the famous Poîlane bakery (No. 8) and the Musée Hébert (No. 85). Main interest ends at the Boulevard Raspail.
✚ G7 Ⓟ Saint-Sulpice

RUE DU FAUBOURG SAINT-HONORÉ
Price tags and politics cohabit in this street of luxury. See Hermès' imaginative window-dressing or salute the gendarmes in front of the Elysée Palace.
✚ F4/5 Ⓟ Madeleine

RUE JACOB
Antique and interior-decoration shops monopolize this picturesque stretch. Make a 20-pace detour to the Musée Delacroix on the delightful Place Furstemberg.
✚ G6 Ⓟ Saint-Germain-des-Prés

RUE MONSIEUR-LE-PRINCE
An uphill stretch lined with university bookshops, antique and ethnic shops, and a sprinkling of student restaurants. Sections of the medieval city wall are embedded in Nos. 41 and 47.
✚ G7 Ⓟ Odéon

RUE DES ROSIERS
Effervescent street at heart of Paris's Jewish quarter. Kosher butchers and restaurants, the old hammam, and Hebrew bookstores rub shoulders with designer boutiques. Quiets considerably on Saturdays.
✚ J6 Ⓟ Saint-Paul

Storefront on the rue des Rosiers

RUE VIEILLE-DU-TEMPLE
The pulse of the hip Marais district, dense in bars, cafés, boutiques, and, farther north, the historic Hôtel Amelot-de-Bisseuil (No. 47), the Maison J Hérouët, the Hôtel de Rohan (No. 87), and the garden of the Musée Picasso (▶ 51).
✚ J6 Ⓟ Saint-Paul

PARIS
where to...

LUXURY HOTELS

Expect to pay over 1,500FF for a single room in the luxury category.

Le Crillon

Whether you stay at the Ritz, the Crillon, the Meurice, the Bristol, or the Georges V, they all have their tales to tell, but that of the Crillon is perhaps the most momentous: this family mansion (still 100 percent French-owned by the Taittingers of champagne fame) managed to survive the Revolution despite having the guillotine on its doorstep. Mary Pickford and Douglas Fairbanks spent their honeymoon here.

LE CRILLON
An old Parisian classic which reeks glamour, history, and major investments. Suites are almost the norm here.
✚ F5 ✉ 10 Place de la Concorde 75008 ☎ 01 44 71 15 00; fax 01 44 71 15 02 🚇 Concorde

L'HÔTEL
A Parisian legend redolent of Oscar Wilde's last days. Kitsch piano-bar and restaurant, and some superb rooms.
✚ G6 ✉ 13 rue des Beaux Arts 75006 ☎ 01 43 25 27 22; fax 01 43 25 64 81 🚇 Saint-Germain-des-Prés

HÔTEL DU JEU DE PAUME
A small, delightful hotel carved out of a 17th-century royal tennis court. Tasteful rooms with beams and marble bathrooms; some duplex suites. No restaurant.
✚ J7 ✉ 54 rue Saint-Louis-en-l'Ile 75004 ☎ 01 43 26 14 18; fax 01 40 46 02 76 🚇 Pont Marie

HÔTEL LUTETIA
Completely refurbished in art deco style by Sonia Rykiel in 1989. Avoid the cheaper back rooms. Well located between Saint-Germain and Montparnasse.
✚ F7 ✉ 45 Boulevard Raspail 75006 ☎ 01 49 54 46 46; fax 01 49 54 46 00 🚇 Sèvres-Babylone

HÔTEL MEURICE
Classically ornate luxury, once home to Salvador Dali and before that the Nazi HQ during the Occupation. Now efficiently run by the CIGA group.
✚ G5 ✉ 228 rue de Rivoli 75001 ☎ 01 44 58 10 10; fax 01 44 58 10 15/16 🚇 Tuileries

HÔTEL MONTALEMBERT
A fashionable Left Bank hotel with a garden-patio, bar, and restaurant. Chic design details and well-appointed rooms. Popular with Americans.
✚ F6 ✉ 3 rue de Montalembert 75007 ☎ 01 45 49 68 68; fax 01 45 49 69 49 🚇 Rue du Bac

HÔTEL SAINTE BEUVE
Exclusive establishment between the heart of Montparnasse and the Luxembourg gardens. Period antiques mix happily with modern furnishings.
✚ G7 ✉ 9 rue Sainte-Beuve 75006 ☎ 01 45 48 20 07; fax 01 45 48 67 52 🚇 Vavin

HÔTEL SAN RÉGIS
Convenient for the couturiers on Avenue Montaigne. Elaborately decorated but modestly scaled hotel, popular with American show-biz folk. Restaurant for hotel guests only.
✚ E5 ✉ 12 rue Jean Goujon 75008 ☎ 01 44 95 16 16; fax 01 45 61 05 48 🚇 Alma-Marceau

PAVILLON DE LA REINE
Set back from Place des Vosges. Flowery courtyard, tasteful period decoration, and comfortable rooms.
✚ J6 ✉ 28 Place des Vosges, 75004 ☎ 01 42 77 96 40; fax 01 42 77 63 06 🚇 Chemin Vert

MID-RANGE HOTELS

HÔTEL DE L'ABBAYE SAINT GERMAIN

This quaint, historic establishment was once a monastery. Flowery, cobbled courtyard, elegant salons, terraced duplex rooms, and friendly staff.

✚ G7 ✉ 10 rue Cassette 75006 ☎ 01 45 44 38 11; fax 01 45 48 07 86 🚇 Saint-Sulpice

HÔTEL D'ANGLETERRE

Former British Embassy. Pretty garden-patio, spacious rooms where Hemingway once stayed. Bar and piano lounge. Book well ahead.

✚ G6 ✉ 44 rue Jacob 75006 ☎ 01 42 60 34 72; fax 01 42 60 16 93 🚇 Saint-Germain-des-Prés

HÔTEL BERGÈRE

A 131-room hotel run by Best Western close to the Grands Boulevards. Reliable though anonymous service.

✚ H4 ✉ 34 rue Bergère 75009 ☎ 01 47 70 34 34; fax 01 47 70 36 36 🚇 Rue Montmartre

HÔTEL DUC DE SAINT-SIMON

Rather pricey but the antique furnishings and picturesque setting just off Boulevard Saint-Germain justify it. Comfortable rooms, intimate atmosphere. Needs advance booking.

✚ F6 ✉ 14 rue Saint-Simon 75007 ☎ 01 45 48 35 66; fax 01 45 48 68 25 🚇 Rue du Bac

HÔTEL LENOX

Popular with the design and fashion world. Chase T. S. Eliot's ghost and enjoy the restored, stylish 1930s bar. Book well ahead.

✚ G6 ✉ 9 rue de l'Université 75007 ☎ 01 42 96 10 95; fax 01 42 61 52 83 🚇 Rue du Bac

HÔTEL DES MARRONIERS

Named after the chestnut trees that dominate the garden. Obsessively vegetal/floral-based decoration. Oak-beamed rooms; vaulted cellars converted to lounges. Book well ahead.

✚ G6 ✉ 21 rue Jacob 75006 ☎ 01 43 25 30 60; fax 01 40 46 83 56 🚇 Saint-Germain-des-Prés

HÔTEL MOLIÈRE

On a quiet street near the Louvre and Opéra. Well-appointed, reasonably priced rooms, and helpful staff.

✚ G5 ✉ 21 rue Molière 75001 ☎ 01 42 96 22 01; fax 01 42 60 48 68 🚇 Pyramides

HÔTEL LA PERLE

Renovated 17th-century building on a quiet street near Saint-Germain. Charming breakfast patio, bar, and well-appointed rooms.

✚ G6 ✉ 14 rue des Canettes 75006 ☎ 01 43 29 10 10; fax 01 46 34 51 04 🚇 Mabillon

RÉSIDENCE LORD BYRON

Comfortable, classy 31-room hotel just off the Champs-Elysées. Small garden and well-appointed, reasonably priced rooms.

✚ E4 ✉ 5 rue Châteaubriand 75008 ☎ 01 43 59 89 98; fax 01 42 89 46 04 🚇 Georges V

A moderately priced hotel will charge 500–1,000FF for a single room.

Three-star rating

All these three-star establishments are obvious favorites with business travelers, so it is virtually impossible to find rooms during trade-fair seasons such as May–early June and mid-September–October. In summer many offer discounts as their clientele shrinks. All rooms are equipped with color TV, direct-dial phone, private bath or shower rooms, minibar, and most with hair dryer. Air-conditioning is not standard, but elevators are common.

BUDGET ACCOMMODATIONS

You should be able to find a single room in a budget hotel for under 500FF.

Budget hotels

Gone are the heady days when Paris was peppered with atmospheric one-star hotels with their inimitable signs *"eau à tous les étages"* ("water on every floor"). Now there are bath or shower rooms in every bedroom, and correspondingly higher prices and smaller rooms. So don't expect much space in budget hotel rooms, but do expect breakfast and receptionists who speak a second language in every hotel with two or more stars.

GRAND HÔTEL MALHER
Recently renovated family hotel with 31 well-equipped rooms; excellent location.
✚ J6 ✉ 5 rue Malher 75004 ☎ 01 42 72 60 92; fax 01 42 72 25 37 🚇 Saint-Paul

GRAND HÔTEL DE SUEZ
Fifty-room hotel in central location on busy boulevard. Good value but lacks atmosphere.
✚ H6 ✉ 31 Boulevard Saint-Michel 75005 ☎ 01 46 34 08 02; fax 01 40 51 79 44 🚇 Cluny-La Sorbonne

HÔTEL ANDRÉ GILL
Charming courtyard setting on quiet side street close to Pigalle. Renovated rooms, reasonably priced.
✚ G3 ✉ 4 rue André Gill 75018 ☎ 01 42 62 48 48; fax 01 42 62 77 92 🚇 Pigalle

HÔTEL DU COLLÈGE DE FRANCE
Tranquil 29-roomed establishment near the Sorbonne. Some 6th-floor rooms offer a glimpse of Notre-Dame.
✚ H7 ✉ 7 rue Thénard 75005 ☎ 01 43 26 78 36; fax 01 46 34 58 29 🚇 Maubert-Mutualité

HÔTEL ESMERALDA
Very popular dollhouse hotel near Notre-Dame. Reasonably priced; book well ahead.
✚ H6 ✉ 4 rue Saint-Julien-le-Pauvre 75005 ☎ 01 43 54 19 20; fax 01 40 51 00 68 🚇 Saint-Michel

HÔTEL ISTRIA
Legendary Montparnasse hotel once frequented by Rilke, Duchamp, and Man Ray. Twenty-six atmospheric rooms and friendly staff.
✚ G8 ✉ 29 rue Campagne Première 75014 ☎ 01 43 20 91 82; fax 01 43 22 48 45 🚇 Raspail

HÔTEL JARDIN DES PLANTES
Pretty hotel overlooking the botanical gardens. Good facilities
✚ H7 ✉ 5 rue Linné 75005 ☎ 01 47 07 06 20; fax 01 47 07 62 74 🚇 Jussieu

HÔTEL KENSINGTON
Convenient for the Eiffel Tower and Champ de Mars. An upscale address for a pleasant little hotel with fully renovated rooms.
✚ E6 ✉ 79 Avenue de la Bourdonnais 75007 ☎ 01 47 05 74 00; fax 01 47 05 25 81 🚇 Ecole-Militaire

HÔTEL LINDBERGH
Modernized hotel on a tranquil side street near busy crossroads and the shops of Saint-Germain. Well-equipped rooms and polyglot staff.
✚ F7 ✉ 5 rue Chomel 75007 ☎ 01 45 48 35 53; fax 01 45 49 31 48 🚇 Sèvres-Babylone

HÔTEL LION D'OR
Small family hotel with adequately modernized rooms and very helpful staff. Good value for its central location.
✚ G5 ✉ 5 rue de la Sourdière 75001 ☎ 01 42 60 79 04; fax 01 42 60 09 14 🚇 Tuileries

HÔTEL MICHELET-ODÉON
Reasonable rates and quiet location next to

Théâtre de l'Odéon. No frills, but helpful service.
➕ G7 ✉ 6 Place de l'Odéon 75006 ☎ 01 46 34 27 80; fax 01 46 34 55 35 Ⓜ Odéon

HÔTEL DE LA PLACE DES VOSGES

Charming 17th-century townhouse in a quiet street close to Place des Vosges. Basic comforts, excellent location.
➕ J6 ✉ 12 rue Birague 75004 ☎ 01 42 72 60 46; fax 01 42 72 02 64 Ⓜ Bastille

HÔTEL PRIMA-LEPIC

In cleaner air up the hill of Montmartre, this bright hotel has well-decorated but smallish rooms and a courtyard-style reception area.
➕ G3 ✉ 29 rue Lepic 75018 ☎ 01 46 06 44 64; fax 01 46 06 66 11 Ⓜ Abbesses

HÔTEL RÉCAMIER

Tranquil, friendly little hotel close to Saint-Germain and the Luxembourg gardens.
➕ G7 ✉ 3 bis Place Saint-Sulpice 75006 ☎ 01 43 26 04 89 Ⓜ Saint-Sulpice

HÔTEL DE ROUEN

Very cheap 22-room hotel with surprisingly well-equipped rooms. Central location near the Louvre and Palais-Royal.
➕ G5 ✉ 42 rue Croix-des-Petits-Champs 75001 ☎ 01 42 61 38 21 Ⓜ Louvre-Rivoli

HÔTEL DU 7E ART

Cinephile's hotel decorated with movie photos and memorabilia. Great location in the Marais and reasonably priced rooms.
➕ J6 ✉ 20 rue Saint-Paul

75004 ☎ 01 42 77 04 03; fax 01 42 77 69 10 Ⓜ Saint-Paul

HÔTEL SOLFÉRINO

A rare budget hotel in the chic 7th. Antique furniture. Opposite Musée d'Orsay on quiet street. Excellent value.
➕ F6 ✉ 91 rue de Lille 75007 ☎ 01 47 05 85 54; fax 01 45 55 51 16 Ⓜ Solférino

HÔTEL DE LA SORBONNE

On a quiet side street near the Sorbonne. Small but comfortable rooms. Well established and unpretentious.
➕ H7 ✉ 6 rue Victor-Cousin 75005 ☎ 01 43 54 58 08; fax 01 40 51 05 18
Ⓜ Cluny-la Sorbonne

HÔTEL DU VIEUX SAULE

On a quiet street north of Marais. Modernized, with reasonable facilities.
➕ J5 ✉ 6 rue de Picardie 75003 ☎ 01 42 72 01 14; fax 01 40 27 88 21
Ⓜ Filles du Calvaire

SUPER HÔTEL

Near Père Lachaise cemetery. Good value, easy transportation, comfortable rooms.
➕ M5 ✉ 208 rue des Pyrénées 75020 ☎ 01 46 36 97 48; fax 01 46 36 26 10
Ⓜ Gambetta

TIMHÔTEL LE LOUVRE

One of small chain with reliable amenities and reasonably priced rooms. Well situated for Louvre and Les Halles.
➕ G5 ✉ 4 rue Croix-des-Petits-Champs 75001 ☎ 01 42 60 34 86; fax 01 42 60 10 39 Ⓜ Louvre-Rivoli

Bed and breakfast

Bed-and-breakfast systems now exist to fix up visitors with host families. Try France Lodge (☎ 01 53 20 02 54; fax 01 53 20 01 25) or International Café Couette (☎ 01 42 94 92 00; fax 01 42 94 93 12). For those who want to stay longer and rent furnished accommodations, the best source is the free classified ads magazine *France-USA Contacts* (*FUSAC*). It is available at English bookshops and student travel agencies.

65

EXPENSIVE RESTAURANTS

The restaurants on the following pages are in three price categories:

$$$ over 400FF per person
$$ up to 400FF per person
$ up to 120FF per person

French mean cuisine

"The only cooks in the civilized world are French. Other races have different interpretations of food. Only the French mean *cuisine* because their qualities—rapidity, decision-making, tact—are used. Who has ever seen a foreigner succeed in making a white sauce?"

—Nestor Roqueplan (1804–1870), Editor of *Le Figaro*.

Rose-tinted dining

Le Pré Catalan ($$$) has an elegant setting near the rose gardens of the Parc Bagatelle, and both indoor and outdoor seating. It serves dishes based on seasonal ingredients and has some exquisite desserts (✉ Bois de Boulogne, Route de Suresnes 75016 ☎ 01 44 14 41 14).

ALAIN DUCASSE ($$$)
This temple of Parisian *nouvelle cuisine* is masterminded by chef Alain Ducasse from Monaco.
✚ C5 ✉ 59 Avenue Raymond Poincaré 75116 ☎ 01 47 27 12 27 ◷ Closed Sat–Sun, Jul ◉ Trocadéro

LE BRISTOL ($$$)
Uniquely elegant 18th-century oval-shaped restaurant, renowned for exquisite seafood and impeccable service.
✚ E4 ✉ 112 rue du Faubourg Saint-Honoré 75008 ☎ 01 42 66 91 45 ◷ Daily ◉ Miromesnil

LE GRAND VEFOUR ($$$)
Superb late-18th century setting under arcades of Palais-Royal, with ghosts of Napoleon, Colette and Sartre. Classic French cuisine. Relatively reasonably priced lunch menu.
✚ G5 ✉ 17 rue du Beaujolais 75001 ☎ 01 42 96 56 27 ◷ Closed Sat–Sun, Aug ◉ Palais-Royal/Musée du Louvre

GUY SAVOY ($$$)
One of Paris's top young chefs continues to surprise with contrasting flavors and textures. Efficient service and contemporary décor.
✚ D4 ✉ 18 rue Troyon 75017 ☎ 01 43 80 40 61 ◷ Closed Sat–Sun ◉ Charles de Gaulle-Etoile

LASSERRE ($$$)
A favorite with foreign visitors for impeccable service and cuisine. An extra is the sliding roof.
✚ E5 ✉ 17 Avenue Franklin-D. Roosevelt 75008 ☎ 01 43 59 53 43 ◷ Closed Sun, Mon lunch, Aug ◉ Franklin-D. Roosevelt

LUCAS-CARTON ($$$)
The beautiful art nouveau décor attracts the dressy rich and famous. Try the roast pigeon with coriander.
✚ F5 ✉ 9 Place de la Madeleine 75008 ☎ 01 42 65 22 90 ◷ Closed Sat–Sun, Aug, 24 Dec–3 Jan ◉ Madeleine

MICHEL ROSTANG ($$$)
Rostang still holds his own in the Parisian gastronomy stakes with interesting combinations, superb cheeses, and desserts. Elegant table settings.
✚ D3 ✉ 20 rue Rennequin 75017 ☎ 01 47 63 40 77 ◷ Closed Sun ◉ Ternes

TAILLEVENT ($$$)
Intimate restaurant with a confirmed reputation—advance booking is essential. Inventive cuisine—try the curried ravioli snails. Superlative wine list.
✚ E4 ✉ 15 rue Lamennais 75008 ☎ 01 44 95 15 01 ◷ Closed Sat–Sun, Aug, public holidays ◉ Georges V

LA TOUR D'ARGENT ($$$)
Legendary sanctuary of *canard au sang* but lighter dishes do exist. Fabulous view over the Ile Saint-Louis, warm atmosphere, and great wine cellar.
✚ H7 ✉ 15–17 Quai de la Tournelle 75005 ☎ 01 43 54 23 31 ◷ Closed Mon ◉ Maubert-Mutualité

REGIONAL FRENCH RESTAURANTS

AUBERGE BRESSANE ($/$$)
Delectable dishes from eastern France, and an impressive wine list of Bordeaux and Burgundies. Mock medieval setting. Excellent-value lunch menus.

✚ E6 ✉ 16 Avenue de la Motte Picquet 75007 ☎ 01 47 05 98 37 ⓒ Closed Sat lunch Ⓜ Latour-Maubourg

LA BARACANE ($$)
Tiny, tastefully decorated restaurant whose menu homes in on Gascony and duck. The set meals are reasonably priced but offer limited choice.

✚ J6 ✉ 38 rue des Tournelles 75004 ☎ 01 42 71 43 33 ⓒ Closed Sat lunch, Sun Ⓜ Bastille

BRASSERIE FLO ($$)
Spectacular Alsatian brasserie which dishes up mountains of delicious *choucroute spéciale*. Noisy, popular and chaotic.

✚ H4 ✉ 7 Cour des Petites Ecuries 75010 ☎ 01 42 46 15 80 ⓒ Daily until 1AM Ⓜ Château d'Eau

LE CAVEAU DU PALAIS ($$)
A long-time favorite with Yves Montand and Simone Signoret. Homey regional cooking.

✚ G6 ✉ 17/19 Place Dauphine 75001 ☎ 01 43 26 04 28 ⓒ Closed Sat, Sun Ⓜ Pont Neuf

CHEZ BENOIT ($$$)
Longstanding favorite, serving classic regional dishes. Reserve ahead.

✚ H5 ✉ 20 rue Saint-Martin 75004 ☎ 01 42 72 25 76 ⓒ Daily Ⓜ Rambuteau

LE CLODENIS ($$)
Intimate, discreet restaurant with a menu of aromatic Provençal dishes.

✚ G2 ✉ 57 rue Caulaincourt 75018 ☎ 01 46 06 20 26 ⓒ Closed Sun–Mon Ⓜ Lamarck-Caulaincourt

LE COUDE FOU ($$)
Popular Marais bistro with hearty classics. Excellent wine list.

✚ J6 ✉ 12 rue du Bourg Tibourg 75004 ☎ 01 42 77 15 16 ⓒ Closed Sun lunch Ⓜ Hôtel de Ville

LE CROQUANT ($$)
Reworks classic dishes of the southwest. Sublime *confit de canard*.

✚ C8 ✉ 28 rue Jean-Maridor 75015 ☎ 01 45 58 50 83 ⓒ Closed Sun eve, Mon Ⓜ Lourmel

AUX FINS GOURMETS ($$)
Copious portions of Basque and Béarnais cuisine in a setting of somewhat faded 1920s splendor.

✚ F6 ✉ 213 Boulevard Saint-Germain 75007 ☎ 01 42 22 06 57 ⓒ Closed Sun, Mon lunch Ⓜ Rue du Bac

LOUIS LANDES ($$)
A warm atmosphere, and a menu of traditional dishes from the southwest. Monthly dinners based round a theme; wine tastings.

✚ F9 ✉ 157 Avenue du Maine 75014 ☎ 01 45 43 08 04 ⓒ Closed Sat lunch, Sun Ⓜ Mouton-Duvernet

Alsace and the southwest

Gastronomically speaking, Alsace and the southwest are probably the best-represented regions in Paris. Numerous brasseries churn out *choucroute* (sauerkraut), but it is the southwest that carries off the prizes with its variations on goose and duck. Recent research has found that inhabitants of this region have unexpectedly low rates of cardiac disease—despite their daily consumption of cholesterol-high *foie gras*.

ASIAN & ITALIAN RESTAURANTS

ASIAN

L'AFGHANI ($)
Tucked away in the heights of Montmartre. Wonderfully authentic Afghan food.

🚩 H3 ✉ 16 rue Paul-Albert 75018 ☎ 01 42 51 08 72 🕐 Daily ⓂChâteau Rouge

BHAI BHAI SWEETS ($)
In a dilapidated covered passageway in the hub of Paris's Little India. The food isn't as spicy-hot as it could be, but the curries are tasty.

🚩 H4 ✉ 77 Passage Brady 75010 ☎ 01 42 46 77 29 🕐 Daily Ⓜ Strasbourg Saint-Denis

CHEZ ROSINE ($$)
Succulent, imaginative dishes orchestrated by charismatic Rosine Ek from Cambodia. Sophisticated.

🚩 G5 ✉ 12 rue du Mont Thabor 75001 ☎ 01 49 27 09 23 🕐 Closed Sun, Mon lunch Ⓜ Tuileries

CHIENG-MAI ($$)
Elegant Thai restaurant with charming service and subtle food—try fish steamed in banana leaf or grilled spicy mussels.

🚩 H7 ✉ 12 rue Frédéric-Sauton 75005 ☎ 01 43 25 45 45 🕐 Closed Sun, part of Aug Ⓜ Maubert-Mutualité

HAWAÏ ($)
Huge, animated canteen-style restaurant, popular with local Chinese. Generous soups, Southeast Asian specialties.

🚩 J10 ✉ 87 Avenue d'Ivry 75013 ☎ 01 45 86 91 90 🕐 Daily Ⓜ Porte d'Ivry

KAPPA ($$)
Children-friendly *sushi* restaurant with a warm, animated atmosphere.

🚩 G6 ✉ 6 rue des Ciseaux 75006 ☎ 01 43 26 33 31 🕐 Closed Sun Ⓜ Saint-Germain-des-Prés

LAO SIAM ($)
Varied Southeast Asian cuisines: try jumbo shrimp sautéed in ginger and chives, or whole crab cooked in coconut milk and chilli pepper.

🚩 K4 ✉ 49 rue de Belleville 75011 ☎ 01 40 40 09 68 🕐 Daily Ⓜ Belleville

LE NIOULLAVILLE ($)
Vast Hong Kong-style restaurant with a long menu of Chinese, Laotian, Thai, and Vietnamese specialties.

🚩 K4 ✉ 32–4 rue de l'Orillon 75011 ☎ 01 43 38 95 23 🕐 Closed Sun evening Ⓜ Belleville

PATTAYA ($)
Unpretentious Thai, with outside tables in summer. Delicious shrimp and lemon-grass soup.

🚩 H5 ✉ 29 rue Etienne-Marcel 75001 ☎ 01 42 33 98 09 🕐 Daily Ⓜ Les Halles

PHÖ DONG-HUONG ($)
Bustling Vietnamese "canteen" which serves generous portions of soup, seafood, and meat. Distinct smoking and no-smoking sections.

🚩 K4 ✉ 14 rue Louis Bonnet 75011 ☎ 01 43 57 42 81 🕐 Closed Tue Ⓜ Belleville

The 13th *arrondissement*

The Parisian Chinese community is spread through Belleville, where it coexists with Arabs and Africans; through the 3rd *arrondissement*, where invisible sweatshops churn out cheap leather goods; and above all through the 13th *arrondissement* (Ⓜ Tolbiac, Porte d'Ivry). At the latter, Chinese New Year is celebrated with dragon parades in late January or early February. Gastronomically speaking the area offers a fantastic array of Indochinese and Chinese restaurants and soup kitchens—all at budget prices.

TAN DINH ($$)
Vietnamese cuisine, in an elegantly designed restaurant situated just behind the Musée d'Orsay. Impressive wine list and polished service.
✚ F6 ✉ 60 rue de Verneuil 75007 ☎ 01 45 44 04 84
🕪 Closed Sun 🚇 Rue du Bac

YAMAMOTO ($)
Super-fresh *sushi* with excellent-value set lunches. Crowded until 2PM, but less animated in the evening.
✚ G5 ✉ 6 rue Chabanais 75002 ☎ 01 49 27 96 26
🕪 Closed Sun 🚇 Bourse

YUGARAJ ($$)
One of Paris's best Indian restaurants. Discreet and elegant, with friendly Sri Lankan waiters and an excellent-value "Delhi-Express" lunch menu.
✚ G6 ✉ 14 rue Dauphine 75006 ☎ 01 43 26 44 91
🕪 Closed Mon lunch 🚇 Pont Neuf

ITALIAN

CASA BINI ($$)
Chic but relaxed, a favorite with Catherine Deneuve. Carpaccio and Tuscan dishes are specialties.
✚ G6 ✉ 36 rue Grégoire de Tours 75006 ☎ 01 46 34 05 60
🕪 Closed Sat, Sun lunch 🚇 Odéon

L'ENOTECA ($$)
Colorful Italian restaurant/wine bar in the Marais district. The *antipasto* buffet is delicious and the pasta dishes are refined.
✚ J6 ✉ 25 rue Charles V 75004 ☎ 01 42 78 91 44
🕪 Daily 🚇 Saint-Paul

PASTAVINO ($)
Bresaola and a choice of three fresh pasta dishes every day. Clean, contemporary design and cheerful service.
✚ G6 ✉ 55 rue Dauphine 75006 ☎ 01 46 33 93 83
🕪 Daily 🚇 Odéon

SIPARIO ($$)
Theatrically styled restaurant convenient for Bastille Opera house. Inventive pasta, seafood, and meat dishes.
✚ K7 ✉ 69 rue de Charenton 75011 ☎ 01 43 45 70 26
🕪 Closed Sun 🚇 Bastille

STRESA ($$)
Fashionable isn't the word. Local couturiers drop in here for a quick pasta or risotto, or an excellent *antipasto*. Run with gusto by Neapolitan identical twins. Book ahead.
✚ E5 ✉ 7 rue de Chambiges 75008 ☎ 01 47 23 51 62
🕪 Closed Sat, Sun 🚇 Alma-Marceau

AUX TROIS CANETTES ($$)
Friendly and old-fashioned establishment plastered with nostalgic views of Naples. Extensive menu of Italian classics—polenta, ossobucco, sardines.
✚ G6 ✉ 18 rue des Canettes ☎ 01 44 07 03 02 🕪 Closed Sat lunch, Sun 🚇 Mabillon

Panini reigns

It is said that Cathérine de Médicis, the Italian wife of Henri II, invented French cuisine in the 16th century—though Gallic opinions may differ. Italian cuisine in 20th-century Paris is, not surprisingly, very much a pizza-pasta affair, and authentic dishes are rare. However, the latest In snack fashions is the toasted *panini*, oozing mozarella and tomatoes, especially popular with businessmen near the Bourse (Stock Exchange).

ARAB RESTAURANTS

Couscous and tajine

Couscous is a mound of steamed semolina which is accompanied by a tureen of freshly cooked vegetables (onion, tomato, carrot, potato, zucchini) and the meat (or not) of your choice, from grilled lamb kabobs (*brochettes*) to chicken or *merguez* (spicy sausages). *Tajine* is a delicious all-in-one stew, traditionally cooked in a covered terracotta dish, which may combine lamb and prunes or chicken, pickled lemon, and olives.

AL DAR ($$)
Luxurious but over air-conditioned restaurant, highly regarded by the Lebanese community. Takeout section.
✚ H7 ✉ 8/10 rue Frédéric Sauton 75005 ☎ 01 43 25 17 15 ⊕ Daily
Ⓜ Maubert-Mutualité

L'ATLAS ($$)
Fabulous kitsch juxtaposition of Louis XIII chairs and Moroccan mosaics. Twelve types of *couscous*, pigeon, and other specialties come with genuine smiles.
✚ H7 ✉ 12 Boulevard Saint-Germain 75005 ☎ 01 46 33 86 98 ⊕ Daily
Ⓜ Maubert-Mutualité

CAFÉ MODERNE ($)
Generous *couscous* and *tajines* as well as basic steaks and fish, and a choice of North African and French wines. 1930s décor.
✚ K6 ✉ 19 rue Keller 75011 ☎ 01 47 00 53 62 ⊕ Closed Sun Ⓜ Bastille

LES CÈDRES DU LIBAN ($)
A Lebanese institution with reasonable prices, friendly service, and excellent *taboulé*, hummus, and spicy meat dishes.
✚ F7 ✉ 5 Avenue du Maine 75014 ☎ 01 42 22 35 18 ⊕ Daily
Ⓜ Montparnasse-Bienvenue

CHEZ OMAR ($)
Generous *couscous* and grilled meats in a friendly, spacious and buzzing setting. Popular,

so book for dinner or arrive early.
✚ J5 ✉ 47 rue de Bretagne 75003 ☎ 01 42 72 36 26 ⊕ Closed Sun lunch Ⓜ Arts et Métiers

DARKOUM ($$)
Refined Moroccan cuisine—seafood, *pastilla*, *couscous*, and *tajines*—served in a spacious Arabian Nights-style setting.
✚ G5 ✉ 44 rue Sainte-Anne 75002 ☎ 01 42 96 83 76 ⊕ Closed Sat lunch Ⓜ Bourse

LE MANSOURIA ($$)
Elegant décor and aromatic *tajines*—and too-large crowds on Saturdays.
✚ L7 ✉ 11 rue Faidherbe 75011 ☎ 01 43 71 00 16 ⊕ Closed Sun, Mon lunch Ⓜ Faidherbe-Chaligny

NOURA ($$)
Stylish, busy Lebanese snack bar with takeout service, brother of the plush Pavillon Noura (☎ 01 47 20 33 33) down the road.
✚ D4 ✉ 27 Avenue Marceau 75116 ☎ 01 47 23 02 20 ⊕ Daily Ⓜ Charles de Gaulle-Etoile

TIMGAD ($$$)
Spectacular Moorish décor. Delicate *pastilla*, perfect *couscous*, attentive service. Reserve ahead.
✚ D4 ✉ 21 rue Brunel 75017 ☎ 01 45 74 23 70 ⊕ Daily Ⓜ Argentine

BRASSERIES & BISTROS

LE BALZAR ($$)

Fashionable brasserie near the Sorbonne. Seafood, pigs' trotters, *cassoulet*. Camus and Sartre had their last argument here.

🔲 H7 ✉ 49 rue des Ecoles 75005 ☎ 01 43 54 13 67 🕐 Closed Aug 🚇 Cluny-La Sorbonne

BOFINGER ($$)

Claims to be Paris's oldest brasserie (1864). Soaring glass dome, lots of mirrors, and chandeliers. Seafood, *choucroute*, and steaks.

🔲 K6 ✉ 5 rue de la Bastille 75004 ☎ 01 42 72 87 82 🕐 Daily 🚇 Bastille

BRASSERIE STELLA ($$)

Original 1950s décor in heart of the chic 16th *arrondissement*. Seafood, oysters, and wines from Sancerre and Beaujolais.

🔲 C5 ✉ 133 Avenue Victor Hugo 75016 ☎ 01 47 27 60 54 🕐 Daily 🚇 Victor Hugo

CHEZ PAUL ($$)

A mecca for Bastille art-dealers and artists, with delicious stuffed rabbit and *steak tartare* but mediocre service. Essential to book.

🔲 K6 ✉ 13 rue de Charonne 75011 ☎ 01 47 00 34 57 🕐 Daily 🚇 Ledru-Rollin

LA COUPOLE ($$)

A Montparnasse institution dating from the 1920s. Wide choice of brasserie food, reasonable late-night menu (after 11PM).

🔲 F7 ✉ 102 Boulevard du Montparnasse 75014 ☎ 01 43 20 14 20 🕐 Daily 🚇 Vavin

LE DROUOT ($)

Art deco canteen belonging to the more famous Chartier (along the road). It is far easier to find a table here and the food is equally good value.

🔲 G5 ✉ 103 rue de Richelieu 75002 ☎ 01 42 96 68 23 🕐 Daily 🚇 Richelieu-Drouot

LE GRAND COLBERT ($$)

Restored 19th-century brasserie opening on to the Galerie Colbert. Good seafood and a cheerful atmosphere.

🔲 G5 ✉ 2 rue Vivienne 75002 ☎ 01 42 86 87 88 🕐 Daily 🚇 Bourse

AU PETIT RICHE ($$)

Wonderful old 1880s bistro. Reliable traditional cuisine and good Loire wines.

🔲 G4 ✉ 25 rue Le Peletier 75009 ☎ 01 47 70 68 68 🕐 Closed Sun 🚇 Richelieu-Drouot

LE PETIT SAINT-BENOÎT ($)

Popular old Saint-Germain classic; décor barely changed since the 1930s. Outside tables in summer.

🔲 G6 ✉ 4 rue Saint-Benoît 75006 ☎ 01 42 60 27 92 🕐 Closed Sat, Sun 🚇 Saint-Germain-des-Prés

AU VIEUX CHÊNE ($)

Pleasantly aged bistro east of the Bastille. Excellent-value traditional dishes, friendly service.

🔲 L7 ✉ 7 rue du Dahomey 75011 ☎ 01 43 71 67 69 🕐 Closed Sun 🚇 Faidherbe-Chaligny

La Coupole

Horror struck Parisian hearts in the mid-1980s when it was announced that La Coupole had been bought by property developers and several floors were to be added on top. This happened, but the famous old murals (by Juan Gris, Soutine, Chagall, Delaunay, and many more) have been reinstated, the red-velvet seats preserved, and the art deco lights duly restored. The 1920s interior is now a historic monument.

SALONS DE THÉ

Mariage-Frères

It's hard to escape from the Mariage-Frères tea shop without making a minor investment in its tastefully presented products—whether a decorative can of obscure Japanese green tea, a Chinese teapot, a tea brick, or a delicately tea-scented candle. The Mariage brothers started importing tea to France back in 1854. The choice now extends to over 400 varieties, so that reading the list of teas on offer becomes an exotic excursion through India to the Far East.

ANGÉLINA ($$)

Lunch is overpriced and overrated, but exquisite cakes and hot chocolate make it a favorite for tea. Proustian Belle Epoque décor.

☐ G5 ☒ 226 rue de Rivoli 75001 ☎ 01 42 60 82 00
◷ Closed evenings, Aug
Ⓜ Tuileries

BERNARDAUD ($$)

Fashionable tea room designed by Olivier Gagnère. The tea and cakes are served on Limoges porcelain.

☐ F4 ☒ 8 bis Galerie Royale 75008 ☎ 01 42 66 22 55
◷ Mon–Sat 8:30AM–7PM
Ⓜ Madeleine

LES ENFANTS GÂTÉS ($)

Comfortable armchairs, plants, and pictures. Good choice of teas, fruit juices, salads, tarts, and cakes. Fills up fast for brunches on weekends.

☐ J6 ☒ 43 rue des Francs-Bourgeois 75004 ☎ 01 42 77 07 63 ◷ Daily until 7:30PM
Ⓜ Rambuteau

LADURÉE ($$)

Tea and cakes under a ceiling fresco of a cherubic pastry chef. Current success builds on an illustrious past and the proximity of luxury shops. Avoid the overpriced lunches.

☐ F5 ☒ 18 rue Royale 75008 ☎ 01 42 60 21 79 ◷ Closed Sun, Aug Ⓜ Concorde

LE LOIR DANS LA THÉIÈRE ($)

Established local favorite. Good for salads, vegetable tarts, cakes, and plenty of tea and fruit juices.

☐ J6 ☒ 3 rue des Rosiers 75004 ☎ 01 42 72 90 61
◷ Daily until 7PM
Ⓜ Saint-Paul

MARIAGE-FRÈRES ($$)

Chic, discreet tea shop with an elegant upstairs tea room perfect for nonsmoking tête-à-têtes over tasty cakes or Sunday brunch. Its sibling is in the Marais (☒ 30/32 rue du Bourg Tibourg 75004 ☎ 01 42 72 28 11).

☐ G6 ☒ 13 rue des Grands Augustins 75006 ☎ 01 40 51 82 50 ◷ Daily until 7:30PM
Ⓜ Odéon

LA PAGODE ($)

Exotic tea room attached to an extraordinary cinema housed in an ornate Chinese pagoda. Overlooks a small Japanese garden.

☐ F6 ☒ 57 bis rue de Babylone 75007 ☎ 08 36 68 75 07 ◷ Afternoons daily
Ⓜ Saint-François-Xavier

A PRIORI THÉ ($$)

A favorite with the fashion crowd. Book at lunch. Light lunches, teas, and cakes.

☐ G5 ☒ 36 Galerie Vivienne 75002 ☎ 01 42 97 48 75
◷ Daily until 7PM Ⓜ Bourse

TCH'A ($)

Sells 40 varieties of Chinese tea and serves delicious light lunches. Traditional service, attractive décor.

☐ G6 ☒ 6 rue du Pont de Lodi 75006 ☎ 01 43 29 61 31
◷ Closed Mon Ⓜ Pont Neuf

MISCELLANEOUS RESTAURANTS

MA BOURGOGNE ($$)

Hearty, unpretentious food perfect for a summer lunch or dinner. Or just stop for a drink.
✚ J6 ✉ 19 Place des Vosges 75004 ☎ 01 42 78 44 64 🕐 Daily. Closed Feb 🚇 Chemin Vert

CAFÉ DE L'INDUSTRIE ($)

Spacious, relaxed café-restaurant-tea room open until 1:30AM with reasonable though basic food. 1970s atmosphere, rock music.
✚ K6 ✉ 16 rue Saint-Sabin 75011 ☎ 01 47 00 13 53 🕐 Closed Sat 🚇 Bastille

AUX CHARPENTIERS ($$)

Solid French cuisine in a popular neighborhood restaurant dedicated to the carpenters' guild. Daily specialties.
✚ G6 ✉ 10 rue Mabillon 75006 ☎ 01 43 26 30 05 🕐 Daily 🚇 Mabillon

LA GALERIE ($)

Pleasant relief from the Montmartre tourist haunts. Very good-value set lunch and dinner menus may include salmon ravioli or duck with cherries. Cheerful and friendly.
✚ G3 ✉ 16 rue Tholozé 75018 ☎ 01 42 59 25 76 🕐 Closed Sun 🚇 Abbesses

JOE ALLEN ($)

Reliable hamburger-based fare served with humor and background music in a still fashionable late-night haunt in Les Halles.
✚ H5 ✉ 30 rue Pierre Lescot 75001 ☎ 01 42 36 70 13 🕐 Daily 🚇 Etienne-Marcel

ORESTIAS ($)

Brash, lively, Greek restaurant with an amazing chandelier. Good value—especially the giant shoulder of lamb.
✉ G6 ✉ 4 rue Grégoire de Tours 75006 ☎ 01 43 54 62 01 🕐 Closed Sun 🚇 Odéon

LA POTÉE DES HALLES ($/$$)

Famed for its delicious *potée* (stewed meat and vegetables) and other regional dishes. Exceptional Belle Epoque interior.
✚ H5 ✉ 3 rue Etienne-Marcel 75001 ☎ 01 42 36 18 68 🕐 Closed Sat lunch, Sun 🚇 Etienne-Marcel

PRUNIER ($$$)

Glamorous clientele, splendid art deco setting, and excellent fresh seafood specialties, prepared under the accomplished eye of a former Taillevent director.
✚ D4 ✉ 16 Avenue Victor Hugo 75016 ☎ 01 44 17 35 85 🕐 Closed Sun eve, Mon 🚇 Charles de Gaulle-Etoile

WILLI'S WINE BAR ($$)

Cheerful, British-owned restaurant/wine bar with an extensive international wine list and fresh French cuisine. Try their sublime Cambridge dessert.
✚ G5 ✉ 13 rue des Petits Champs 75001 ☎ 01 42 61 05 09 🕐 Closed Sun 🚇 Palais-Royal/Musée du Louvre

Pharamond

Alexandre Pharamond served his first plate of *tripes à la mode de Caen* in 1870, two doors from the site of the present restaurant, a sanctuary for lovers of tripe, pigs' trotters, and *andouillette*. It was entirely redecorated for the 1900 Exposition Universelle, and most of this structure and decoration has been preserved. The pretty floral and vegetal friezes which cover the walls of the rooms once adorned the entire four-floor façade. Prices are high and booking is essential (✚ H5 ✉ 24 rue de la Grande Truanderie 75001 ☎ 01 42 33 06 72 🕐 Closed Mon lunch, Sun, Jul 🚇 Les Halles).

DEPARTMENT STORES & DESIGNER BOUTIQUES

DEPARTMENT STORES

BHV (BAZAR DE L'HÔTEL DE VILLE)

The do-it-yourself mecca. Browse among the basement nuts and bolts, choose paint or have wood cut on the 5th floor.

✚ H6 ✉ 52/64 rue de Rivoli 75004 ☎ 01 42 74 90 00 ⊙ Mon–Tue, Thu–Sat 9:30–7; Wed 9:30AM–10PM ⊜ Hôtel de Ville

AU BON MARCHÉ RIVE GAUCHE

Very *BCBG* (*bon chic bon genre*). Gourmet foods, designer clothes, household linens, and haberdashery. Excellent basement bookstore.

✚ F7 ✉ 22 rue de Sèvres 75007 ☎ 01 44 39 80 00 ⊙ Mon–Sat 9:30–7 ⊜ Sèvres-Babylone

GALERIES LAFAYETTE

Under a giant glass dome, an enticing display of everything a home and its inhabitants need. Marginally better quality and pricier than Printemps. Top fashion designers are all represented and accessories are endless. Smaller branch near the Tour Montparnasse.

✚ G4 ✉ 40 Boulevard Haussmann 75009 ☎ 01 42 82 34 56 ⊙ Mon–Wed, Fri–Sat 9:30–6:45; Thu 9:30–9 ⊜ Chaussée d'Antin

MARKS & SPENCER

Food, clothes, household goods, and excellent wines. Another branch of this very British chain-store is at 35 Boulevard Haussmann 75009.

✚ H6 ✉ 88 rue de Rivoli 75004 ☎ 01 44 61 08 00 ⊙ Mon–Fri 10–8; Sat 10–7:30 ⊜ Châtelet, Hôtel de Ville

PRINTEMPS

A classic for men's and women's fashions, accessories, household goods, furniture, designer gadgets, and more. Budget-conscious fashion-victims should look for the store's own collection: Sélection Printemps.

✚ G4 ✉ 64 Boulevard Haussmann 75009 ☎ 01 42 82 50 00 ⊙ Mon–Wed, Fri–Sat 9:35–7; Thu 9.35AM–10PM ⊜ Havre-Caumartin

SAMARITAINE

Labyrinthine department store largely occupying a superb 1904 construction. Fashion is so-so, but the toy department is great. Good basement hardware section, and a useful separate store for sports equipment and clothes.

✚ H6 ✉ 19 rue de la Monnaie 75001 ☎ 01 40 41 20 20 ⊙ Mon–Wed, Fri–Sat 9:30–7; Thu 9:30AM–10PM ⊜ Pont Neuf

DESIGNER BOUTIQUES

AGNÈS B

Pioneering designer who now rests on her comfortable reputation; still a favorite for her unchanging classics. Her shops monopolize most of this street. Children's and men's clothes too.

Opening hours

Parisian opening hours follow a Monday–Saturday pattern. Smaller shops generally open by 10AM, sometimes closing for lunch, and shut at 7PM. Avoid shopping on Saturdays, when every citizen seems to hit the streets, and take advantage of department store late-opening nights. Chain stores such as Prisunic and Monoprix are useful when you need inexpensive household goods and even fashion accessories.

✚ H5 ✉ 1–6 rue du Jour
75001 ☎ 01 45 08 56 56
Ⓜ Les Halles

AMELIA MENDES
Interesting fabrics and
cuts as well as young
and chic label by KYO
who also designs for
Dior and Scherrer at
much less affordable
prices.
✚ G5 ✉ 8 rue de la Vrillière
75001 ☎ 01 42 61 07 30
Ⓜ Bourse

BARBARA BUI
One of Paris's most
talented young
designers. You'll find
silky flowing fabrics in
subtle colors, well-cut
suits, and a superb
setting by Pucci de
Rossi.
✚ G5 ✉ 23 rue
Etienne-Marcel 75001 ☎ 01 40
26 43 65 Ⓜ Etienne-Marcel

CHANTAL THOMASS
Paris's sexiest clothes
shop, suspiciously
reminiscent of an
upscale brothel.
Stockings, lacey
lingerie, and some
equally seductive
clothes.
✚ G5 ✉ 1 rue Vivienne
75001 ☎ 01 40 15 01 36
Ⓜ Bourse

DOROTHÉE BIS
Classically imaginative
knitwear in colorful,
supple styles, popular
with a more mature,
avant-garde clientèle.
✚ H5 ✉ 46 rue
Etienne-Marcel 75002 ☎ 01 42
21 04 00 Ⓜ Les Halles

IRIÉ
A former Kenzo assistant
creates superbly cut and
accessibly priced
separates. A pioneer on
this discreet street.
✚ G6 ✉ 8 rue du Pré-aux-
Clercs 75007 ☎ 01 42 61 18
28 Ⓜ Saint-Germain-des-Prés

KASHIYAMA
Look out for the label of
Martin Margiela, a rising
star from Antwerp who
worked for Gaultier and
now designs his own
version of the avant-
garde.
✚ G6 ✉ 147 Boulevard
Saint-Germain 75006
☎ 01 46 34 11 50
Ⓜ Saint-Germain-des-Prés

LOLITA LEMPICKA
Established inventive
chic, very Parisienne.
Ultrafeminine details
and shop design.
✚ J6 ✉ 3 bis rue des Rosiers
75004 ☎ 01 42 74 42 94
Ⓜ Saint-Paul

MICHEL KLEIN
Reliably chic from
season to season. Search
out the Klein d'Oeil
label, which offers very
feminine designs for
budgets that are smaller
(but not tiny).
✚ G6 ✉ 6 rue du Pré-aux-
Clercs 75007 ☎ 01 47 03 93
76 Ⓜ Saint-Germain-des-Prés

ROMEO GIGLI
Venetian carnival
invades an old printers'
workshop. Gigli's rich
velvet, taffeta, silk, and
jersey designs are
presented like works of
art, which they are.
Men's creations on
mezzanine.
✚ J6 ✉ 46 rue de Sévigné
75004 ☎ 01 48 04 57 08
Ⓜ Saint-Paul

Fashion hubs
The fact that women's high
fashion is concentrated in just
three epicenters makes clothes
shopping, or mere window-
gazing, easy. The hub of Place
des Victoires (home to Kenzo,
Stephane Kélian, Plein Sud, and
Victoire) continues along the rue
Etienne-Marcel and towards Les
Halles. The Marais's enticing
offerings run between the rue de
Sévigné, rue des Rosiers, Place
des Vosges, and side streets.
Saint-Germain burgeons along
and off the boulevard, rue de
Grenelle, and continues up the
Boulevard Raspail.

Zen cuts
Issey Miyake reigns OK! His
sculptural, finely pleated
creations in imaginative
synthetics are sold at 3 Place des
Vosges 75004 (☎ 01 48 87 01
86), but Plantation/Issey Miyake
at 17 Boulevard Raspail 75007
(☎ 01 45 48 12 32) is where
more accessible designs are
available. If black and white is
your style, head for Yohji
Yamamoto at 25 rue du Louvre
75001 (☎ 01 42 21 42 93) for
sober geometric cuts for men and
women.

MARKETS

Food markets

Parisians shop daily for their ultra-fresh produce and perfectly ripe cheeses. Temporary food markets spring up on boulevards throughout the city on different days of the week (the Bastille Sunday market is particularly enormous), but permanent food markets exist on rue Poncelet (🚇 D3), rue Daguerre (🚇 G/F8), and on rue de Buci on the Left Bank (🚇 G6). All keep provincial lunch hours, so avoid 1–4PM.

CARREAU DU TEMPLE
A covered market specializing in leather goods. Bargain hard and you may pay half the usual price.
🚇 J5 ✉ Rue E. Spuller 75003 🕐 Tue–Sun 9–noon 🚇 Temple

MARCHÉ D'ALIGRE
Secondhand clothes, crockery and bric-a-brac huddle in the middle of a large, low-priced food market.
🚇 K7 ✉ Place d'Aligre 75012 🕐 Tue–Sun 8–1 🚇 Ledru-Rollin

MARCHÉ DE MONTREUIL
Jeans and jackets start at the métro. Persevere across the bridge for domestic appliances, carpets, bric-a-brac, and some great secondhand stuff. Morning is best.
🚇 N6 ✉ Avenue de la Porte de Montreuil 75020 🕐 Sat–Mon 7–6 🚇 Porte de Montreuil

MARCHÉ AUX OISEAUX
Caged birds whistle and chirp for new owners every Sunday. During the week (except Mon) you'll find a flower market.
🚇 H6 ✉ Place Louis Lépine 75004 🕐 Sun 9–7 🚇 Cité

MARCHÉ AUX PUCES DE SAINT-OUEN
(➤ 42)

MARCHÉ DE LA RUE LEPIC
Up a steep hill, but worth the effort. Head down the other side of the hill to the rue du Poteau (🚇 G/H2 🚇 Jules-Joffrin) for African foods.
🚇 G3 ✉ Rue Lepic 75018 🕐 Tue–Sat 9–1, 4–7; Sun 9–1 🚇 Abbesses

MARCHÉ DE LA RUE MONTORGUEIL
The leftovers of Les Halles food market, now a marble-paved pedestrian street with atmosphere and plenty of trendy little bars and lunch places.
🚇 H5 ✉ Rue Montorgueil 75001 🕐 Tue–Sat 9–1, 4–7; Sun 9–1 🚇 Les Halles

MARCHÉ DE LA RUE MOUFFETARD
A tourist classic straggling down a winding, hilly street. Wonderful array of fruit and vegetables, and plenty of aromatic cheeses and charcuterie. Good café stops *en route*.
🚇 H8 ✉ Rue Mouffetard 75005 🕐 Tue, Thu, Sat 9–1, 4–7 🚇 Monge

MARCHÉ AUX TIMBRES
Philatelists zoom in here to buy and sell.
🚇 E5 ✉ Rond-Point des Champs-Elysées 75008 🕐 Thu, Sat, Sun and holidays 9–7 🚇 Franklin-D. Roosevelt

MARCHÉ DE VANVES
A favorite with young yuppies hot on 1950s and deco styles. Secondhand furniture, bric-a-brac, paintings, prints, and some ethnic items.
🚇 E9 ✉ Avenue Georges Lafenestre, Avenue Marc Sangnier 75014 🕐 Sat–Sun 7–7:30 🚇 Porte de Vanves

ART & ANTIQUES

ARTCURIAL

Large store of contemporary art (prints, jewelry, sculpture, carpets). An excellent art bookstore is on site.
🔢 E4 ✉ 9 Avenue Matignon 75008 ☎ 01 42 99 16 16 🕐 Tue–Sat 10:30–7:15 🚇 Franklin-D. Roosevelt

CARRÉ RIVE GAUCHE

This grid of streets is home to some of Paris's top antique dealers. Archaeological pieces, Louis XIV, XV, Empire, Japanese scrolls, astrolabes, prints—it's all here.
🔢 G6 ✉ Rue du Bac, Quai Voltaire, rue des Saints-Pères, rue de l'Université 75007 🕐 Tue–Sat 10:30–7 🚇 Rue du Bac

GALERIE DOCUMENTS

Original posters and etchings from 1890 to 1940 by such masters as Toulouse-Lautrec and Mucha.
🔢 G6 ✉ 53 rue de Seine 75006 ☎ 01 43 54 50 68 🕐 Tue–Sat 10:30–12:30, 2:30–7 🚇 Odéon

GALERIE DURAND-DESSERT

Spectacular conversion of an old Bastille mattress factory into a conceptual art mecca.
🔢 K6 ✉ 28 rue de Lappe 75011 ☎ 01 48 06 92 23 🕐 Tue–Sat 11–7 🚇 Bastille

GALERIE DU JOUR AGNÈS B

Fashion meets art at Agnès B's gallery, with young, hip talent on view in photography and painting.
🔢 H5 ✉ 6 rue du Jour 75001 ☎ 01 42 33 43 40 🕐 Tue–Sat 11–7 🚇 Les Halles

GALERIE MONTENAY

A longstanding contemporary art gallery, where young French and foreign artists are regularly exhibited.
🔢 G6 ✉ 31 rue Mazarine 75006 ☎ 01 43 54 85 30 🕐 Tue–Sat 11–1, 2:30–7 🚇 Odéon

LOUVRE DES ANTIQUAIRES

Huge, modernized complex of antique shops. You'll find everything from Eastern carpets to Lalique glass, jewelry, furniture, silver, porcelain, and paintings. High prices.
🔢 G5 ✉ 2 Place du Palais-Royal 75001 ☎ 01 42 97 27 00 🕐 Tue–Sun 11–7 🚇 Palais-Royal/Musée du Louvre

VILLAGE SAINT-PAUL

A cluster of antique and bric-a-brac shops opening onto an enclosed square. Shops continue down the streets on either side, with everything from Asian textiles to glass, old furniture or clothes.
🔢 J6 ✉ Rue Saint-Paul, rue Charlemagne 75004 🕐 Thu–Mon 11–7 🚇 Saint-Paul

VILLAGE SUISSE

Network of upscale furniture and antique shops in a chic residential area.
🔢 D7 ✉ 54 Avenue de la Motte-Piquet, 78 Avenue de Suffren 75015 ☎ 01 43 06 69 90 🕐 Thu–Sun 10:30–7 🚇 La Motte-Piquet

Galleries

Even if you cannot afford to invest in contemporary art, Paris offers a good window on the latest movements. Art has traditionally centered on the Left Bank around the rue de Seine, but today the more avant-garde galleries spread east from the Centre Georges Pompidou area through the Marais to the Bastille. Pick up a free gallery map at one of the galleries and follow the creative route.

BOOKS & RECORDS, DESIGN & INTERIOR, FOOD & WINE

Sunday openings

Sundays now have a strong consumer itch to them at the new marble-clad Carrousel du Louvre, perfect for a rainy day. Offerings include a Virgin record/bookstore, a newsagent with a wide international selection, Bodum kitchenware, Nature et Découvertes (a fashionably "ecological" toy and gadget shop), a stylish optician, and various boutiques. The entrance is from 99 rue de Rivoli or by the Carrousel arch in the Louvre.

BOOKS & RECORDS

BRENTANO'S

Well-stocked American bookstore with good travel and art sections at the back. Bilingual staff.
✚ G5 ✉ 37 Avenue de l'Opéra 75001 ☎ 01 42 61 52 50 Ⓜ Opéra

LA CHAMBRE CLAIRE

Excellent photography bookstore with a wide range of international publications. Occasional exhibitions.
✚ G7 ✉ 14 rue Saint-Sulpice 75006 ☎ 01 46 34 04 31 ⏱ Mon–Sat Ⓜ Odéon

FNAC

The main branch of this firmly established cultural chain. Books, records, cameras, audio, computer accessories. Fair-price policy reigns and staff are helpful.
✚ G7 ✉ 136 rue de Rennes 75006 ☎ 01 49 54 30 00 Ⓜ Saint-Sulpice

GALIGNANI

Pleasantly traditional, spacious bookstore brimming with laden tables and shelves. Large stock of English, German, and French literature and art books.
✚ G5 ✉ 224 rue de Rivoli 75001 ☎ 01 42 60 76 07 Ⓜ Tuileries

LA HUNE

Excellent literary bookstore with extensive art and architecture section. Both French and imported books. Great for late-night browsing—doors open weekdays until midnight.
✚ G6 ✉ 170 Boulevard Saint-Germain 75006 ☎ 01 45 48 35 85 Ⓜ Saint-Germain-des-Prés

LIBRAIRIE DES FEMMES

A feminist bookstore with a vast choice of international women writers. Next to the Saint-Germain market.
✚ G7 ✉ 74 rue de Seine 75006 ☎ 01 43 29 50 75 Ⓜ Odéon

VIRGIN MEGASTORE

Enormous palace of records with generous opening hours, plus a chic café. Another branch is in the Carrousel du Louvre, 99 rue de Rivoli (✚ G5).
✚ E4 ✉ 52/60 Champs-Elysées 75008 ☎ 01 49 53 50 00 ⏱ Mon–Thu 10AM–midnight; Fri–Sat 10AM–1AM; Sun noon–midnight Ⓜ Franklin-D. Roosevelt

DESIGN & INTERIOR

DEHILLERIN

Food-lover's paradise, brimming with copper pans, knives, bains-maries, sieves and more. Mail-order service.
✚ H5 ✉ 18 rue de la Coquillière 75001 ☎ 01 42 36 53 13 Ⓜ Les Halles

EN ATTENDANT LES BARBARES

Colorful hive of primitive-baroque designer objects, from resin candlesticks to funky furniture by young French designers.
✚ H5 ✉ 50 rue Etienne-Marcel 75001 ☎ 01 42 33 37 87 Ⓜ Sentier

ETAMINE

Vast home-interior shop with superb objects and fabrics imported from all over the world, but firmly stamped with Parisian taste.

F6 ✉ 63 rue du Bac 75007 ☎ 01 42 22 03 16 ⓢ Rue du Bac

SOULEIADO

Cheerful range of fabrics, table linen, and cushions in bright, sunny Provençal prints.

G6 ✉ 78 rue de Seine 75006 ☎ 01 43 54 62 25 ⓢ Mabillon

FOOD & WINE

ANDROUET

Encyclopedic range of pungent French cheeses in perfectly ripened states. Cheese restaurant attached; delivery service in Paris.

F3 ✉ 41 rue d'Amsterdam 75008 ☎ 01 48 74 26 90 ⓢ Liège

FAUCHON

The gourmet's paradise —at a price. Established luxury delicatessen offering only the best in spices, exotic fruit, tea, coffee, charcuterie, pâtisseries…and more.

F5 ✉ 26 Place de la Madeleine 75008 ☎ 01 47 42 60 11 ⓢ Madeleine

IZRAËL

Colorful souk spilling North African and Middle Eastern goodies onto sidewalk. Sacks of grains, bottles of spices, piles of African baskets.

J6 ✉ 30 rue François Miron 75004 ☎ 01 42 72 66 23 ⓢ Saint-Paul

LEGRAND FILLES ET FILS

Fine wines and selected groceries in a shop dating from 1890. Helpful advice, wide price range but reliable quality. Occasional wine tastings.

G5 ✉ 1 rue de la Banque 75002 ☎ 01 42 60 07 12 ⓢ Bourse

LA MAISON DU MIEL

Countless types of honey—chestnut, lavender, pine-tree, acacia—presented in a pretty, tiled interior dating from 1908.

F4 ✉ 24 rue Vignon 75009 ☎ 01 47 42 26 70 ⓢ Madeleine

A LA MÈRE DE FAMILLE

Original 18th-century grocery shop with shelves laden with imaginatively created chocolates, sweets, jams, and unusual groceries.

I14 ✉ 35 rue du Faubourg Montmartre 75009 ☎ 01 47 70 83 69 ⓢ Le Peletier

ROBERT LABEYRIE

Specializes in products from the Landes. Goose and duck livers, *foie gras*, truffles, dried mushrooms of all types.

H5 ✉ 6 rue Montmartre 75001 ☎ 01 45 08 95 26 ⓢ Les Halles

TACHON

Unpretentious old-fashioned cheese shop, renowned for its goat, sheep and cow products.

G5 ✉ 38 rue de Richelieu 75001 ☎ 01 42 96 08 66 ⓢ Palais-Royal/Musée du Louvre

Ethnic attractions

Gourmets suffering from a surfeit of delectable but outrageously priced French groceries should head for Paris's ethnic areas. For Indian products the Passage Brady (H4) is unbeatable, while the nearby rue d'Enghien harbors several Turkish grocery stores. Belleville offers both Arab and Chinese specialties, while the Goutte d'Or (Barbès) focusses on Africa. For a real taste of the Far East, go to the Chinese supermarket Tang Frères at 47 Avenue d'Ivry in the 13th *arrondissement* (J9).

MISCELLANEOUS & OFFBEAT

Window-shopping

Some Parisian streets do not fit any convenient slot and so make for intriguing window-shopping. Try rue Jean-Jacques Rousseau and Passage Véro-Dodat (⊞ G/H5), rue Saint-Roch (⊞ G5), rue Monsieur-le-Prince and parallel rue de l'Odéon (⊞ G7), rue Saint-Sulpice, rue des Francs-Bourgeois and rue du Pont-Louis-Philippe (⊞ J6), or rue de la Roquette (⊞ K/L6). For luxury goods take a stroll along the rue du Faubourg Saint-Honoré (⊞ E4–G5).

ANTHONY PETO
The male answer to Marie Mercié (➤ 81). Inventive and wearable men's quality headgear from top hats to berets, all aimed at the young and hip.
⊞ G5 ✉ 12 rue Jean-Jacques Rousseau 75001 ☎ 01 42 21 47 15 Ⓜ Louvre-Rivoli

LES ARCHIVES DE LA PRESSE
Old magazines, newspapers, and catalogues.
⊞ J6 ✉ 51 rue des Archives 75003 ☎ 01 42 72 63 93 Ⓜ Rambuteau

L'ART DU BUREAU
High-tech and designer accessories for the desk top, tasteful stationery.
⊞ J6 ✉ 47 rue des Francs Bourgeois 75004 ☎ 01 48 87 57 97 Ⓜ Saint-Paul

AXIS
Witty contemporary objects, plates, teapots, jewelry, and clocks. Another shop is at the Bastille, 13 rue de Charonne (⊞ K6).
⊞ G6 ✉ 18 rue Guénégaud 75006 ☎ 01 43 29 66 23 Ⓜ Odéon

CHÉRI-BIBI
Amusing and inventive women's hats at very affordable prices. Bit of a trek but worth it.
⊞ K6 ✉ 82 rue de Charonne 75011 ☎ 01 43 70 51 72 Ⓜ Charonne

CHRISTIAN TORTU
Anemones, amaryllis, and apple-blossom...this is the place for the ultimate bouquet. Wrapping is in understated brown paper bound with raffia.
⊞ G6 ✉ 6 Carrefour de l'Odéon 75006 ☎ 01 43 26 02 56 Ⓜ Odéon

CUISINOPHILE
Tiny little shop packed with decorative old kitchen utensils, mostly in working order.
⊞ J6 ✉ 28 rue du Bourg Tibourg 75004 ☎ 01 40 29 07 32 Ⓜ Hôtel de Ville

DEBAUVE & GALLAIS
Original wood-paneled 18th-century pharmacy, which became a chocolate shop when the medicinal properties of cocoa were discovered.
⊞ G6 ✉ 30 rue des Saints-Pères 75007 ☎ 01 45 48 54 67 Ⓜ Saint-Germain-des-Prés

DIDIER LUDOT
Rare vintage designer clothes (Chanel, Dior, Balmain), and classic Hermès handbags. Picturesque location.
⊞ G5 ✉ 24 Galerie Montpensier 75001 ☎ 01 42 96 06 56 Ⓜ Palais-Royal/Musée du Louvre

DIPTYQUE
For over 30 years this boutique has sold its own perfumed candles and *eaux de toilette*, plus men's ties, scarves, and superb glasses.
⊞ H7 ✉ 34 Boulevard Saint-Germain 75005 ☎ 01 43 26 45 27 Ⓜ Maubert-Mutualité

L'HABILLEUR
Leftover designer stock at huge discounts. Plenty of choice, with helpful sales staff.
⊞ J5 ✉ 44 rue de Poitou 75003 ☎ 01 48 87 77 12 Ⓜ Saint-Sébastien-Froissart

IKUO

A tiny little shop packed with interesting jewelry, mainly by Japanese creators. Good value.

🕂 G6 ✉ 11 rue des Grands Augustins 75006 ☎ 01 43 29 56 39 🚇 Pont Neuf

JEAN LAPORTE

An aromatic universe of potpourris, essences, candles, and perfumes based on floral, fruity, and spicy themes.

🕂 F6 ✉ 84 bis rue de Grenelle 75007 ☎ 01 45 44 61 57 🚇 Rue du Bac

MARIE MERCIÉ

Extravagant hats. Choose your headgear here or in her original shop near Les Halles at 56 rue Tiquetonne (🕂 H5).

🕂 G7 ✉ 23 rue Saint-Sulpice 75006 ☎ 01 43 26 45 83 🚇 Mabillon

MI-PRIX

Designer clothes at a fraction of the price; also shoes by Michel Perry.

🕂 C8 ✉ 27 Boulevard Victor 75015 ☎ 01 48 28 42 48 🚇 Porte de Versailles

MOUTON À CINQ PATTES

Cut-price designer clothes packed into a crowded shop. Another branch is at 15 rue Vieille du Temple (🕂 J6).

🕂 G6 ✉ 19 rue Grégoire des Tours 75006 ☎ 01 43 29 73 56 🚇 Odéon

NAÏLA DE MONBRISON

Gallery showing some of the most sought-after contemporary jewelry

designers' work: Marcial Berro, Tina Chow, Mattia Bonetti.

🕂 F6 ✉ 6 rue de Bourgogne 75007 ☎ 01 47 05 11 15 🚇 Varenne

PAPIER +

Wonderful emporium of quality paper in endless subtle hues. Superbly bound books, files, and bouquets of colored pencils.

🕂 J6 ✉ 9 rue du Pont Louis-Philippe 75004 ☎ 01 42 77 70 49 🚇 Pont Marie

SCOOTER

To get that real Les Halles look, drop in here for the latest accessories: ethnic, 1960s/70s revival transformed into jewelry, bags, clothes.

🕂 H5 ✉ 10 rue de Turbigo 75001 ☎ 01 45 08 89 31 🚇 Les Halles

SI TU VEUX

Charming toystore with affordable and interesting toys, games and dressing-up gear. Separate section devoted to teddy-bear-related items.

🕂 G5 ✉ 68 Galerie Vivienne 75002 ☎ 01 42 60 59 97 🚇 Bourse

TATI

Originally aimed at the emptiest purses in Paris, Tati now attracts the rich and famous but is still low cost. Women's men's, and children's clothes, as well as household goods.

🕂 H3 ✉ 2–30 Boulevard Rochechouart 75018 ☎ 01 42 55 13 09 🚇 Barbès-Rochechouart

Chocaholics

Chocolate came to Europe via Spain from South America. Under Louis XIV it became a fashionable drink and was served three times a week at Versailles. Paris's first chocolate shop opened in 1659. Voltaire drank up to 12 cups a day, and Napoleon apparently had a penchant for it first thing in the morning. But with their consumption of a mere 12lb. per person per annum, the French lag behind the Swiss, who consume an annual 22lb., and the Belgians at 15lb.

CONCERTS, JAZZ CLUBS & NIGHTCLUBS

Inexpensive concerts

Numerous classical music concerts are held in churches—try Saint-Eustache, Saint-Germain-des-Prés, Saint-Julien-le Pauvre, Saint-Louis-en-l'Ile, Saint-Roch, and Saint-Séverin. Seats are reasonably priced and the quality of music is sometimes very high. In May–September free concerts are held in parks all over the city. Programs are available at the Office du Tourisme or the Hôtel de Ville, or ☎ 01 40 71 76 47.

Recitals

Chopin gave his last recital at what is now the most prestigious venue on the classical circuit and home to the Orchestre de Paris—the Salle Pleyel (⊠ 252 rue du Faubourg Saint-Honoré ☎ 01 45 61 53 00). It is the venue for many of Paris's major concerts, often with world-famous soloists, and for radio and record recordings. Another established concert hall, the Salle Gaveau, still attracts top international opera singers and pianists despite its shabby appearance (⊠ 45 rue de la Boétie 75008 ☎ 01 49 53 05 07).

CONCERT VENUES

AUDITORIUM DES HALLES
Lunchtime and early evening concerts and recitals: classical music, world music, jazz.
✚ H5 ⊠ Forum des Halles, Porte Sainte-Eustache 75001 ☎ 01 42 36 13 90 🚇 Les Halles

CITÉ DE LA MUSIQUE
Accessible classical, jazz, and world music at this new concert hall in an out-of-the-way location.
✚ L2 ⊠ 221 Avenue Jean-Jaurès 75019 ☎ 01 44 84 44 84 🚇 Porte de Pantin

OPÉRA BASTILLE
Long-term teething problems continue at Paris's "people's" opera house. Opera, recitals, dance, and even theater.
✚ K6 ⊠ 120 rue de Lyon 75012 ☎ 01 44 73 13 00 🚇 Bastille

OPÉRA COMIQUE
Sumptuously decorated opera house which stages light opera, dance, and sometimes theater.
✚ G4 ⊠ 5 rue Favart 75002 ☎ 01 42 44 45 46 🚇 Richelieu-Drouot

THÉÂTRE DES CHAMPS-ELYSÉES
Top international orchestras play in a stately setting. Expensive.
✚ E5 ⊠ 15 Avenue Montaigne 75008 ☎ 01 49 52 50 50 🚇 Alma-Marceau

THÉÂTRE DU CHÂTELET
Varied program of opera, symphonic music, and dance. Cheap seats for lunchtime.
✚ H6 ⊠ Place du Châtelet 75001 ☎ 01 40 28 28 40 🚇 Châtelet

THÉÂTRE DE LA VILLE
Modern theater with an adventurous program of contemporary dance, avant-garde music, theater, and early evening recitals of world music.
✚ H6 ⊠ Place du Châtelet 75004 ☎ 01 42 74 22 77 🚇 Châtelet

JAZZ CLUBS

BILBOQUET
Traditional jazz, pricey cocktails, and a strait-laced crowd with a good sprinkling of tourists. Restaurant.
✚ G6 ⊠ 13 rue Saint-Benoît 75006 ☎ 01 45 48 81 84 🚇 Saint-Germain-des-Prés

CAVEAU DE LA HUCHETTE
Still going strong, a smoky basement bar with dancing and live jazz from 9:30PM.
✚ H6 ⊠ 5 rue de la Huchette 75005 ☎ 01 43 26 65 05 🚇 Saint-Michel

CHAPELLE DES LOMBARDS
Funky Bastille haunt with a hot atmosphere. Caribbean, raï (Algerian rock), and rap music. Open until dawn.
✚ K6 ⊠ 19 rue de Lappe 75011 ☎ 01 43 57 24 24 🕐 Thu–Sat 🚇 Bastille

NEW MORNING
One of Paris's top jazz/blues/soul bars.

Good atmosphere, dedicated crowd. Book for top names.
✚ H4 ✉ 7/9 rue des Petites Ecuries 75010 ☎ 01 45 23 56 39 Ⓜ Château d'Eau

PETIT OPPORTUN

Classic jazz venue in Les Halles featuring live bands from 10:30PM. Reasonable prices.
✚ H6 ✉ 15 rue des Lavandières-Sainte-Opportun 75001 ☎ 01 42 36 01 36 Ⓒ Closed Sun Ⓜ Châtelet

LE SUNSET

Part of the Les Halles cluster, a restaurant-bar with good jazz from 10PM until the small hours. Reasonably priced food.
✚ H6 ✉ 60 rue des Lombards 75001 ☎ 01 40 26 46 60 Ⓜ Châtelet

LA VILLA

Top jazz names. Sleek cocktail bar in stylish post modern hotel basement, open late. Book.
✚ G6 ✉ 29 rue Jacob 75006 ☎ 01 43 26 60 00 Ⓒ Closed Sun Ⓜ Saint-Germain-des-Prés

NIGHTCLUBS

L'ARC

Fairly upscale club with selective door policy. Piano bar, restaurant, and indoor garden.
✚ D4 ✉ 12 rue de Presbourg, 75016 ☎ 01 45 00 45 00 Ⓒ From 11:30PM nightly Ⓜ Charles de Gaulle-Etoile

LES BAINS

Still number one for the fashion and showbiz set. Heavy door policing— go very late. Restaurant.
✚ H5 ✉ 7 rue du Bourg-l'Abbé 75003 ☎ 01 48 87 01 80 Ⓒ Nightly Ⓜ Etienne-Marcel

LE BALAJO

Over 60 years old with ritzy 1930s décor. The music is mainly disco, techno, and funk.
✚ K6 ✉ 9 rue de Lappe 75011 ☎ 01 47 00 07 87 Ⓒ Thu–Sat Ⓜ Bastille

LE BATACLAN

An old favorite now rejuvenated. You'll find the fashion-media set, with fancy dress on Fridays, mainly house music on Saturdays.
✚ K5 ✉ 50 Boulevard Voltaire 75011 ☎ 01 47 00 30 12, 47 00 55 22 Ⓒ Thu–Sat from 11PM Ⓜ Oberkampf

PIGALL'S

Latest Pigalle haunt which thunders soul, acid-jazz. Transvestites add to the funkiness.
✚ G3 ✉ 77 rue Pigalle 75009 ☎ 01 46 27 82 82 Ⓒ Thu–Sat from 12PM Ⓜ Pigalle

RÉGINE

Flashy mature crowd, rich in media stars. Careful grooming matters, so look neat— you may be lucky.
✚ E4 ✉ 49–51 rue de Ponthieu 75008 ☎ 01 43 59 21 13 Ⓜ Franklin-D. Roosevelt

LE TANGO

Unpretentious club with Afro-Latino rhythms, tango, salsa, reggae, and soul.
✚ J5 ✉ 13 rue au Maire 75003 ☎ 01 42 72 17 78 Ⓒ Fri–Sat from 11PM Ⓜ Arts et Métiers

Clubs and raves

Paris clubbing is both serious and fickle—serious because no truly cool Parisian turns up before midnight, and fickle because mass loyalties change rapidly. Most clubs keep going through the night until dawn on Friday and Saturday nights, and nearly all charge an entry (this usually includes a drink). For impromptu raves, theme nights, and house parties outside Paris, with shuttles provided, check *Pariscope*'s English section or key in to Minitel 3615 Party News.

BARS & SPECIAL CINEMAS

BARS

BAR DU MARCHÉ

A hip watering hole with good sounds and cheerful service. Nice outdoor terrace.

🔲 G6 ✉ 75 rue de Seine 75006 ☎ 01 43 26 55 15 🕐 Daily 8AM–1AM 🚇 Odéon

BAR ROMAIN

Original 1905 décor brightens this bar-restaurant, popular with a more mature showbiz crowd. Choice of over 200 cocktails.

🔲 G4 ✉ 6 rue de Caumartin 75009 ☎ 01 47 42 98 04 🕐 Mon–Sat 12PM–2AM 🚇 Havre-Caumartin

BIRDLAND

An old Saint-Germain favorite. Relaxed atmosphere, with great jazz records.

🔲 G6 ✉ 8 rue Princesse 75006 ☎ 01 43 26 97 59 🕐 Nightly 7PM–6AM 🚇 Mabillon

LES BOUCHONS

Late-night basement bar with occasional live jazz. Cheerful restaurant upstairs.

🔲 H6 ✉ 19 rue des Halles 75001 ☎ 01 42 33 28 73 🕐 Nightly 11:30PM–dawn 🚇 Châtelet

CAFÉ CANNIBALE

World-music sounds in a restored baroque setting in a burgeoning neighborhood near Belleville. Relaxed, spacious, and popular.

🔲 K5 ✉ 93 rue Jean-Pierre Timbaud 75011 ☎ 01 49 29 95 59 🕐 Daily 🚇 Couronnes

CAFÉ CHARBON

Hip café-bar with a mirrored interior. Enjoy the budget snacks or read the papers here until 2AM.

🔲 K5 ✉ 109 rue Oberkampf 75011 ☎ 01 43 57 55 13 🕐 Daily 🚇 Parmentier

CAFÉ NOIR

Packed, late-night haunt on fringe of Les Halles. High-decibel rock and an unmistakable technicolor exterior.

🔲 H5 ✉ 65 rue Montmartre 75002 ☎ 01 40 39 07 36 🕐 Daily 7:30AM–2AM. Closed Sun 🚇 Sentier

LA CASBAH

Moorish-styled bar with dancing, fancily dressed bar staff, great cocktails and décor. Very unfriendly bouncers.

🔲 K7 ✉ 18 rue de la Forge-Royale 75011 ☎ 01 43 71 71 89 🕐 Wed–Sat 11:30PM onwards 🚇 Faidherbe-Chaligny

CHINA CLUB

Hip and crowded red-lacquered bar-restaurant peopled by Mao-style waiters. Avoid the food, go for a drink. Another bar upstairs.

🔲 K7 ✉ 50 rue de Charenton 75012 ☎ 01 43 43 82 02 🕐 Nightly 7PM–2AM 🚇 Ledru-Rollin

HARRY'S BAR

Old pub atmosphere. Rowdy, mature, well-tanked-up crowd.

🔲 G5 ✉ 5 rue Daunou 75002 ☎ 01 42 61 71 14 🕐 Nightly 10:30PM–4AM 🚇 Opéra

JACQUES MÉLAC

Inexpensive French wines by the glass or

Cinephile's paradise

Though French film production dropped below the 100 mark in 1994, the capital is still a cinephile's paradise. With some 350 films shown each day, the choice can be tantalizing. Foreign films shown in their original languages have "*VO*" (*version originale*) after the title. New films come out on Wednesdays, which is also the day for all-round reductions. The Gaumont and UGC cinemas offer multiple-entry cards which can be used for up to three people and save precious francs.

bottled for you from
the barrel.
🚇 L6 ✉ 42 rue Léon Frot
75011 ☎ 01 43 70 59 27
🕐 Closed Sat–Sun and mid-
Jul–mid-Aug Ⓜ Charonne

MAYFLOWER

Lively, reasonably
priced bar-pub that has
attracted student
nighthawks for years.
🚇 H7 ✉ 49 rue Descartes
75005 ☎ 01 43 54 56 47
🕐 Daily 7AM–2AM Ⓜ Cardinal
Lemoine

LE MOLOKO

Cavernous, popular bar
on two floors. Loud—
but you can still talk.
🚇 G3 ✉ 26 rue Fontaine
75009 ☎ 01 48 74 50 26
🕐 Daily 9:30PM–6AM
Ⓜ Blanche

LA TARTINE

An old daytime classic.
French wines by the
glass, cold platters of
charcuterie and cheese.
🚇 J6 ✉ 24 rue de Rivoli
75004 ☎ 01 42 72 76 85
🕐 8:30AM–10PM. Closed Tue and
Aug Ⓜ Hôtel de Ville

LE TRAIN BLEU

Striking Belle Epoque
setting which functions
as restaurant-bar. Food
pricey; stick to drinks.
🚇 K7 ✉ 1st floor, Gare de
Lyon, 75012 ☎ 01 43 43
09 06 🕐 Daily 9AM–11PM
Ⓜ Gare de Lyon

WEB BAR

Funky little cyber café
with art shows, videos,
and music daily until
2AM. Good weekend
brunches.
🚇 J5 ✉ 32 rue de Picardie
75003 ☎ 01 42 72 66 55
🕐 Daily Ⓜ République

SPECIAL CINEMAS

LA CINÉMATHÈQUE FRANÇAISE

Cinema classics, with
foreign films always in
the original language.
🚇 D5 ✉ 7 Avenue Albert de
Mun 75016 ☎ 01 47 04 24 24
Ⓜ Trocadéro

LE DOME IMAX

The world's largest
hemispherical screen
(12,314 square feet).
Digital sound system.
🚇 Off map at A2 ✉ 1 Place
du Dôme, La Défense 92905
☎ 01 46 92 45 45
Ⓜ La Défense

L'ENTREPOT

Stimulating program of
French and foreign
films, plus festivals
devoted to one director.
Bookstore, pleasant café.
🚇 F8 ✉ 7–9 rue Francis de
Pressensé 75014 ☎ 08 36 68
05 87 Ⓜ Pernéty

LA PAGODE

A unique cinema hall
housed inside an exotic
Japanese pagoda.
Adjoining tea room
(► 72) and garden.
🚇 F6 ✉ 57 bis rue de
Babylone 75007 ☎ 01 45 55
48 48 Ⓜ Saint-François Xavier

VIDÉOTHÈQUE DE PARIS

Movies or documentaries
shot in or connected
with Paris, and film
classics. A cheap day
pass admits you to four
different films.
🚇 H5 ✉ Forum des Halles,
Porte Sainte-Eustache 75001
☎ 01 40 26 34 30 Ⓜ Les
Halles

Steambaths

If nocturnal bar-crawling
becomes too much, why not
sweat it out at a steambath? The
hammam at the Mosquée
(► 52) offers a lovely tiled
interior à la Marrakesh
(🕐 Men: Fri and Sun. Women:
Mon, Wed, Thu and Sat). A new
though pricier alternative is Les
Bains du Marais (✉ 31 rue des
Blancs-Manteaux 75004 ☎ 01
44 61 02 02 🕐 Men: Thu and
Sat. Women: Mon–Wed).

SPORTS

Pools and horses

Paris's municipal swimming pools have complicated opening hours which are almost entirely geared to schoolchildren. Phone beforehand to check for public hours and avoid Wednesdays and Saturdays, both favorites with children off school. Gymnase Clubs are generally open until 9PM but close on Sundays. If horse-racing is your passion, don't miss the harness racing at Vincennes with its brilliant flashes of color-coordinated horses and jockeys. Check *Paris-Turf* for race programs.

AQUABOULEVARD
Huge family complex with water-shoots, palm trees, Jacuzzis. Gym, putting greens, tennis and squash courts too—at a price.
➕ C8 ✉ 4–6 rue Louis Armand 75015 ☎ 01 40 60 10 00 🚇 Porte de Versailles

GYMNASE CLUB
Best-equipped gymnasium in this chain. Call for details on other gyms throughout Paris. Day passes, book of ten passes, or annual subscription.
➕ D3 ✉ 17 rue du Débarcadère 75017 ☎ 01 45 74 14 04 🚇 Porte Maillot

HIPPODROME D'AUTEUIL
Flat-racing and hurdles. Hosts the prestigious Prix du Président de la République hurdle race.
➕ A6 ✉ Bois de Boulogne, 75016 ☎ 01 42 24 47 04 🕐 Closed Jul–Aug 🚇 Porte d'Auteuil

HIPPODROME DE LONGCHAMP
Longchamp is where the hats and champagne come out for the annual Prix de l'Arc de Triomphe. Regular flat-races.
➕ Off map at A6 ✉ Bois de Boulogne 75016 ☎ 01 42 24 13 29 🕐 Closed Jul–Aug 🚇 Porte d'Auteuil, then shuttle

HIPPODROME DE VINCENNES
Colorful harness racing pulls in the crowds. Watch out for the Prix d'Amérique, the top harness race of the season.
➕ Off map at N9 ✉ 2 route de la Ferme, Bois de Vincennes 75012 ☎ 01 49 77 17 17 🕐 Closed Jul–Aug 🚇 Château de Vincennes, then shuttle

PARC DES PRINCES
Huge municipal stadium takes 50,000 spectators for major soccer and rugby games.
➕ A8 ✉ 24 rue du Commandant-Guilbaud 75016 ☎ 01 42 88 02 76 🚇 Porte de Saint-Cloud

PISCINE DES HALLES (SUZANNE BERLIOUX)
Underground 50m pool overlooked by lush tropical garden.
➕ H5 ✉ 10 Place de la Rotonde 75001 ☎ 01 42 36 98 44 🚇 Les Halles

PISCINE JEAN TARIS
Two 25m pools with view of Panthéon. Electronically cleaned water, so no chlorine.
➕ H7 ✉ 16 rue Thouin 75005 ☎ 01 43 25 54 03 🚇 Cardinal Lemoine

PISCINE QUARTIER LATIN
A 33m pool with a distinct 1930s air. Solarium, squash courts, gym, and sauna.
➕ H7 ✉ 19 rue de Pontoise 75005 ☎ 01 43 25 31 99 🚇 Maubert-Mutualité

ROLAND-GARROS
Clay-court home to the French Tennis Open. Tickets are sold months ahead but plenty of racketeers sell seats on the day at the main entrance.
➕ A7 ✉ 2 Avenue Gordon-Bennett 75016 ☎ 01 47 43 00 47 🚇 Porte d'Auteuil, then walk or catch bus 32, 52, 123

PARIS
travel facts

ARRIVING & DEPARTING

Before you go

- Visas are not required for EU nationals, or US, or Canadian citizens, but are obligatory for Australians and New Zealanders.
- Anyone entering France must have a valid passport (or official identity card for EU nationals).
- There are no vaccination requirements.

When to go

- Spring rarely starts before mid-May; June is always glorious.
- July and August see the Great Parisian Exodus. Cultural activities move into bottom gear, but lodging is easier.
- Avoid mid-September to mid-October, the peak trade-fair period, when hotels are full.
- Winter temperatures rarely drop below freezing but rain is usual in January and March.

Arriving by train

- The Eurostar train service from London arrives at Gare du Nord ☎ 08 36 35 35 35.
- Trains arrive at the Gare de l'Est from Germany, Austria, and Eastern Europe.
- The Gare de Lyon serves southeast France and Italy, the Gare d'Austerlitz southwest France, Spain, and Portugal.
- The central TGV stations are Gare Montparnasse and Gare de Lyon.
- All stations have métro, bus, and taxi services.
- For reservations and information on SNCF stations ☎ 01 45 82 50 50 (7AM–9PM daily).

Arriving by air

- Air passengers arrive either at

Roissy-Charles de Gaulle airport (14 miles north of Paris) or at Orly (9 miles to the south).
- Taxis charge a surcharge at airports and at stations, and also for each item of luggage carried.

Roissy

- Connections to downtown are: via a direct RER train into Châtelet-Les Halles; the Air France bus which stops at Etoile (Arc de Triomphe) and Porte Maillot; the cheaper Roissybus which terminates at rue Scribe, Opéra.
- The Air France bus and Roissybus run every 15–20 minutes, 5:40AM–11PM.
- Taxis are expensive.
- For passenger information ☎ 01 48 62 22 80.

Orly

- Connections to downtown are via the Air France bus, which goes to Invalides every 12 minutes and stops at Porte d'Orléans, or the more economical Orlybus, which goes to Denfert-Rochereau every 15 minutes.
- Avoid Orlyrail as this involves a shuttle bus.
- For passenger information ☎ 01 49 75 15 15.

Customs regulations

- There are no restrictions on goods brought into France by EU citizens.
- For non-EU nationals the limits are: 200 cigarettes or 100 cigarillos or 50 cigars or 250g of tobacco; 2 liters of wine; 1 liter of spirits; 50g of perfume; 500g of coffee; and 100g of tea.
- Prescribed medicines and up to 50,000FF of currency may be imported.

Departing

- Airport tax for departing passengers is included in the price of your ticket.
- There are numerous duty-free shops at Orly and Roissy airports, but not on Eurostar or other international trains.
- Allow one hour to reach Roissy airport, by any transport means, and 45 minutes for Orly.

ESSENTIAL FACTS

Travel insurance

- Insurance to cover theft, illness, and repatriation is strongly advised.

Opening hours

- Banks: Mon–Fri 9–4:30. Closed on public holidays and often the preceding afternoon.
- Post offices: Mon–Fri 8–7; Sat 8–noon. The central post office (✉ 52 rue du Louvre 75001 ☎ 01 40 28 20 00) provides a 24-hour service for post, telegrams and telephone.
- Shops: Mon–Sat 9–7 or 9:30–6:30, with minor variations (smaller shops close at lunch). Arab-owned groceries stay open until 9 or 10PM, including Sun.
- Museums: national museums close on Tuesday, municipal museums on Monday. Individual opening hours vary considerably; always phone to check hours for national holidays.

National holidays

- January 1, May 1 , May 8 , Ascension (last Thursday in May), Whit Monday (early June), July 14, August 15, November 1, November 11, December 25.
- Sunday services for public transportation operate; many restaurants, large shops, and local groceries disregard national holidays.

Money matters

- The French currency is the franc (FF): 1FF = 100 centimes.

Foreign exchange

- Only banks with *change* signs change foreign currency/ traveler's checks: a passport is necessary. Bureaux de change are open longer hours but rates can be poorer.
- Airport and station exchange desks are open 6:30AM–11PM.
- For late-night exchange in central Paris use the Exchange Corporation ✉ 63 Avenue des Champs-Elysées 75008 ☎ 01 42 56 11 35 🚇 Franklin-D. Roosevelt 🕐 Daily 8AM–noon.

Credit cards

- Credit cards are widely accepted.
- VISA cards (including MasterCard and Diners Club) can be used in cash dispensers. Most machines flash up instructions in the language you choose.
- American Express is less common, so Amex cardholders needing cash should use American Express ✉ 11 rue Scribe 75009 ☎ 01 47 14 50 00 🚇 Opéra.

Etiquette

- Shake hands on introduction and on leaving; once you know people better replace this with a peck on both cheeks.
- Always use *vous* unless the other person breaks into *tu*.
- It is polite to add *Monsieur*, *Madame*, or *Mademoiselle* when addressing strangers or salespeople.

- Always say hello and goodbye in shops.
- When calling waiters, use *Monsieur* or *Madame* (not *garçon*!).
- Dress carefully. More emphasis is put on grooming than in other countries.

Women travelers
- Women are safe to travel alone or together. Deal with any unwanted attention firmly and politely.

Places of worship
- The International Center for Religious Information (✉ 6 Place du Parvis-Notre-Dame 75004 ☎ 01 46 33 01 01 🚇 Saint-Michel), an English-speaking service, supplies information on services and churches for Catholic, Protestant, and Orthodox worshippers.
- Protestant churches: American Church ✉ 65 Quai d'Orsay 75007 ☎ 01 47 05 07 99 🚇 Invalides. St George's English Church ✉ 7 rue Auguste Vacquerie 75016 ☎ 01 47 20 22 51 🚇 Charles de Gaulle-Etoile.
- Jewish: Synagogue ✉ 10 rue Pavée 75004 ☎ 01 42 77 81 51 🚇 Saint-Paul.
- Russian Orthodox: Saint Alexandre de la Néva ✉ 12 rue Daru 75008 ☎ 01 42 27 37 34 🚇 Courcelles.

Student travelers
- An International Student Identity Card reduces cinema charges, entrance to museums, and air and rail travel.
- AJF (Accueil des Jeunes en France) ✉ 119 rue Saint-Martin 75004 ☎ 01 42 77 87 80 🚇 Châtelet 🕐 Mon–Sat 9–6:30. Gives advice on hostel accommodations, and discounts on train tickets.
- CIDJ (Centre d'Information et de Documentation Jeunesse) ✉ 101 Quai Branly 75015 ☎ 01 44 49 12 00 🚇 Bir-Hakeim 🕐 Mon–Fri 10–6. Youth information centre for jobs, courses, sports, etc.

Time differences
- France is six hours ahead of New York. Clocks change at the autumn and spring solstices.

Toilets
- Public toilet booths are common, and are generally well maintained.
- Every café has a toilet, although standards vary. Do not use a cafe's toilet without ordering at least a drink. WCs in museums and restaurants are often better.

Electricity
- Voltage is 220V and sockets take two round pins.

Tourist Information Office
- Office de Tourisme de Paris ✉ 129 Avenue des Champs-Elysees 75008 ☎ 01 49 52 53 54 🕐 9AM–8PM 🚇 Charles de Gaulle-Etoile. Masses of tourist information and polyglot staff.

PUBLIC TRANSPORTATION

Métro
- Métro lines are identified by their terminus (*direction*) and a number; connections are indicated with orange panels marked *correspondances* on the platform.
- Blue *sortie* signs show the exits.
- The first métros run at 5:30AM, and the last around 12:30AM.

- Keep your ticket until you exit—it has to be re-slotted on the RER and ticket inspectors prowl the métro.
- Avoid rush hours: 8–9:30AM and 4:30–7PM.

Bus

- Hail buses from bus stops.
- Enter, and punch your ticket into the machine beside the driver or flash your pass (see below).
- Night buses run hourly 1:30AM–5:30PM from Place du Châtelet out to the *portes* and suburbs.

Tickets and passes

- Tickets and passes function for métro, buses and RER.
- Pass prices and the number of tickets required for a ride depend on how many of five travel zones you intend to pass through.
- A *carnet* of ten tickets is considerably cheaper than individual tickets.
- *Formule 1* is a one-day pass, valid on métro, buses, and RER.
- A *Paris Visite* card gives unlimited travel for three or five days plus discounts at certain monuments.
- The *carte hebdomadaire* pass (photo required) is valid Mon–Sun.
- The *carte orange* pass, also needing a photo, is valid for one calendar month.

Maps

- Free métro/bus/RER maps are available at every station and on some buses.
- RATP information (in French) ☎ 01 43 46 14 14 ⏰ 6AM–9PM.
- RATP tourist office ✉ 53 bis Quai des Grands Augustins 75006 ☎ 01 40 46 42 17.

Taxis

- Taxis can be hailed in the street if the roof sign is illuminated, or they can be found at ranks.
- Sunday and night rates (7PM–7AM) rise considerably and extra charges are made at stations, Air France terminals, for luggage, and for animals.
- Taxi-drivers expect tips of 10 percent.
- Radio-taxi firms: Taxis Bleus (☎ 01 49 36 10 10); Alpha (☎ 01 45 85 85 85); G7 (☎ 01 47 39 47 39); Artaxi (☎ 01 42 41 50 50).

MEDIA & COMMUNICATIONS

Telephones

- Most Parisian phone booths use France Telecom phone cards (*télécarte* for 50 or 120 units), available from post offices, *tabacs*, stations, or at main métro stations. A few booths still use coins, particularly those in cafés.
- Cheap periods for international calls vary: for the USA and Canada, daily 2AM–noon, with lesser reductions 8PM–2AM; for Europe, Australia and New Zealand Mon–Sat 9:30PM–8AM and all day Sun.
- Repairs ☎ 13.
- Information ☎ 12.
- International information ☎ 00 33 12 + country prefix.
- In 1996 French telephone numbers changed to ten digits.
- 00 is now the prefix for international calls.
- All numbers in the Ile-de-France, including Paris, start with 01 unless at extra rates, when they start with 08.
- To call the French provinces, use: 02 Northwest, 03 Northeast, 04 Southeast, 05 Southwest.

Post offices
- Stamps can be bought at *tabacs* and mail posted in any yellow mailbox.
- All post offices have free access to the Minitel directory service, express courier post (Chronopost), phone booths, and photocopying machines.

Press
- The main dailies are *Le Monde* (out at 2PM), *Libération*, and *Le Figaro*.
- Weekly news magazines range from the left-wing *Le Nouvel Observateur*, *L'Express* (center) and *Le Point* (center-right) to *Paris Match* and *Canard Enchaîné*. For weekly listings of cultural events, buy a copy of *Pariscope* (with an English section) or *L'Officiel des Spectacles*.
- Central newspaper kiosks and newsagents stock European dailies.
- The NMPP's central bookstore (✉ 93 rue Montmartre 75002) has a comprehensive range of French and foreign press, while the newsagent in the Carrousel beneath the Louvre carries American press and international fashion publications.

Radio and television
- FM stations run the gamut from current affairs on France Inter (87.8 MHz) to unadulterated rap/rock/house music on Radio Nova (101.5 MHz).
- France 2 and France 3, the state TV channels, occasionally have good documentaries and current events programs. TF1 has lightweight entertainment, and M6 is still evolving. Arte (on Channel 5), a serious Franco-German cultural channel, offers good European coverage.

EMERGENCIES

Precautions
- Watch wallets and handbags as pickpockets are active, particularly in crowded bars, flea markets, and cinemas.
- Keep traveler's-check numbers separate from the checks themselves.
- Make a declaration at a local *commissariat* (police station) to claim losses on your insurance.

Lost property
- The police lost-property office is ✉ 36 rue des Morillons 75015 🕐 8:30AM–5PM Ⓜ Convention. No phone inquiries.

Medicines and medical treatment
- Minor ailments can often be treated at pharmacies (identified by a green cross), where staff will also advise on local doctors.
- All public hospitals have a 24-hour emergency service (*urgences*) as well as specialist doctors. Payment is made on the spot, but if you are hospitalized ask to see the *assistante sociale* to arrange payment directly through your insurance.
- House calls are made with SOS Médecins ☎ 01 47 07 77 77, or for dental problems SOS Dentistes ☎ 01 43 37 51 00.
- 24-hour pharmacy: Dhéry ✉ 84 Avenue des Champs-Elysées 75008 ☎ 01 45 62 02 41.
- The Drug-store chain at Opéra and Champs-Elysées offers pharmacies, newsagents, cafés, and tobacconists open until 2AM.

Emergency phone numbers
- Crisis-line in English: SOS Help ☎ 01 47 23 80 80 🕐 3–11PM.
- Fire (*sapeurs pompiers*) ☎ 18.

- 24-hour ambulance service (SAMU) ☎ 15.
- Police ☎ 17.
- Anti-poison ☎ 01 40 37 04 04.

Embassies and consulates

- US Embassy ✉ 2 Avenue Gabriel 75008 ☎ 01 43 12 22 22.
- US Consulate ✉ 2 rue Saint-Florentin 75001 ☎ 01 42 96 14 88.
- Canadian Embassy ✉ 35 Avenue Montaigne 75008 ☎ 01 44 33 29 00.
- Canadian Consulate ✉ 37 Avenue Montaigne 75008 ☎ 01 44 43 29 16.
- British Embassy ✉ 35 rue du Faubourg Saint-Honoré 75008 ☎ 01 42 66 91 42.
- British Consulate ✉ 9 Avenue Hoche 75008 ☎ 01 42 66 38 10.
- Australian Embassy ✉ 4 rue Jean Rey 75015 ☎ 01 40 59 33 00.
- New Zealand Embassy ✉ 7ter rue Léonard de Vinci 75016 ☎ 01 45 00 24 11.

LANGUAGE

1	un	16	seize
2	deux	17	dix-sept
3	trois	18	dix-huit
4	quatre	19	dix-neuf
5	cinq	20	vingt
6	six	21	vingt-et-un
7	sept	30	trente
8	huit	40	quarante
9	neuf	50	cinquante
10	dix	60	soixante
11	onze	70	soixante-dix
12	douze	80	quatre-vingt
13	treize	90	quatre-vingt-dix
14	quatorze	100	cent
15	quinze	1,000	mille

Basic vocabulary

yes/no oui/ non
please s'il vous plaît

thank you merci
excuse me excusez-moi
hello bonjour
good evening bon soir
goodbye au revoir
how are you? comment allez-vous? ça va?
very well thanks trés bien merci
how much? combien?
do you speak English? parlez-vous anglais?
I don't understand je ne comprends pas
where is/are…? où est/sont…?
here/there ici/là
turn left/right tournez à gauche/droite
straight on tout droit
behind/in front derrière/devant
when? quand?
today aujourd'hui
yesterday hier
tomorrow demain
how long? combien de temps?
at what time? à quelle heure?
what time do you open/close? à quelle heure ouvrez/ fermez-vous?
do you have…? avez-vous…?
a single room une chambre simple
a double room une chambre double
an extra bed un lit supplementaire
with/without bathroom avec/sans salle de bains
breakfast le petit déjeuner
lunch le déjeuner
dinner le dîner
how much is this? c'est combien?
it's expensive/inexpensive c'est cher/pas cher
do you take credit cards? acceptez-vous des cartes de credit?
I need a doctor/dentist j'ai besoin d'un médecin/dentiste
can you help me? pouvez-vous m'aider?
where is the hospital? où est l'hôpital?
where is the police station? où est le commissariat?

INDEX

Citypack
Paris

Copyright   © 1996, 1997 by The Automobile Association
Maps copyright © 1996 by The Automobile Association
Fold-out map: © RV Reise- und Verkehrsverlag Munich · Stuttgart
                        © Cartography: GeoData

Published in the United States by Fodor's Travel Publications, Inc.
Published in the United Kingdom by AA Publishing

Fodor's is a registered trademark of Fodor's Travel Publications, Inc.

ISBN 0-679-00001-1
Second Edition

FODOR'S CITYPACK PARIS

AUTHOR *Fiona Dunlop*
CARTOGRAPHY *The Automobile Association*
RV Reise- und Verkehrsverlag
COVER DESIGN *Tigist Getachew, Fabrizio La Rocca*
COPY EDITOR *Susie Whimster*
VERIFIER *Giselle Thain*
INDEXER *Marie Lorimer*
SECOND EDITION UPDATED BY *OutHouse Publishing Services*

Acknowledgments

The Automobile Association would like to thank the following photographers, picture
libraries and associations for their assistance in the preparation of this book: F Dunlop
44b, 45; The Louvre 35b; Musée Carnavalet 46a; Musée des Arts Décoratifs 34; Musée
Marmottan 24; Rex Features Ltd 9. All remaining pictures are held in the Association's
own library (AA Photo Library), with contributions from: M Adleman 87a; P Enticknap
26b; R Moore 21; D Noble 20; K Paterson 2, 5a, 5b, 6, 25a, 25b, 28a, 28b, 30, 39a, 40,
43a, 52, 53, 56, 60; B Rieger 1, 17, 23a, 32, 44a, 55, 57, 58, 61b; A Souter 7, 13a, 16, 18,
26a, 27, 29, 31a, 31b, 41b, 43b, 48, 49a, 50, 51, 54; W Voysey 13b, 23b, 33a, 35a, 36a,
36b, 41a, 42, 46b, 47, 49b, 59, 61a, 87b.
The author would like to thank Dominique Benedittini, Christophe Boicos and Andrew
Hartley for their help during the preparation of this book.

Special sales

Color separation by Daylight Colour Art Pte Ltd, Singapore
Manufactured by Dai Nippon Printing Co. (Hong Kong) Ltd
10 9 8 7 6 5 4 3

Titles in the Citypack series

● Amsterdam ● Atlanta ● Berlin ● Boston ● Chicago ● Florence ● Hong Kong ●
● London ● Los Angeles ● Miami ● Montréal ● New York ● Paris ● Prague ●
● Rome ● San Francisco ● Tokyo ● Toronto ● Venice ● Washington, D.C. ●